Drainage of Highway Pavements

Federal Highway Administration (FHWA),
Department of Transportation (DOT)

DRAINAGE OF HIGHWAY PAVEMENTS

Hydraulic Engineering
Circular No. 12

FHWA-TS-84-202

March 1984

U.S. Department
of Transportation

**Federal Highway
Administration**

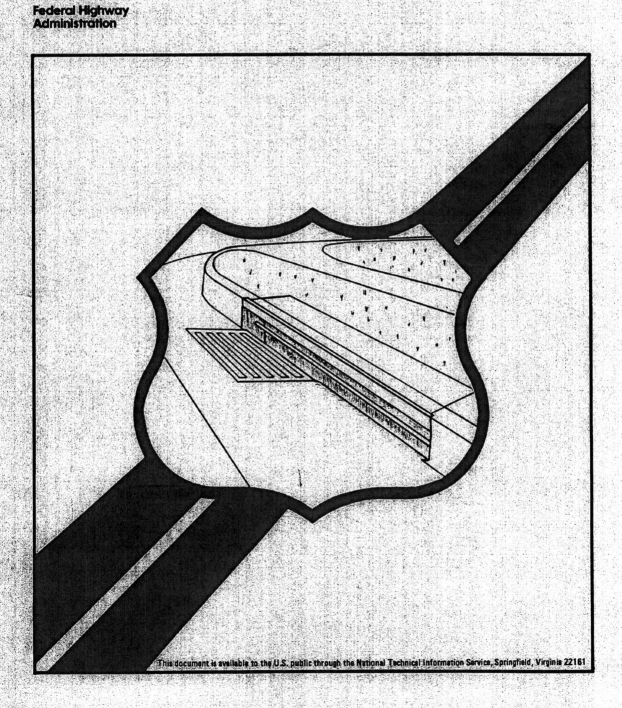

FOREWORD

This Technology Sharing Report provides guidelines and design procedures for the drainage of highway pavements. The guidelines should be of interest to roadway and hydraulic design engineers. Safety specialists concerned with grate inlets and pavement spread will also find this manual useful.

The report was prepared by Tye Engineering, Inc. with technical guidance from the FHWA Office of Engineering's Hydraulics Branch (HNG-31).

Sufficient copies of the publication are being distributed to provide a minimum of one copy to each FHWA region office, division office, and to each State highway agency. Additional copies will be available to public agencies from the FHWA Office of Engineering (HNG-31).

D. K. Phillips
Director
Office of Engineering

R. J. Betsold
Director
Office of Implementation

NOTICE

This document is disseminated under the sponsorship of the Department of Transportation in the interest of information exchange. The United States Government assumes no liability for its contents or use thereof. The contents of this report reflect the views of the contractor, who is responsible for the accuracy of the data presented herein. The contents do not necessarily reflect the official views or policy of the Department of Transportation. This report does not constitute a standard, specification or regulation.

The United States Government does not endorse products or manufacturers. Trade or manufacturers' names appear herein only because they are considered essential to the object of this document.

1. Report No. HEC No. 12 FHWA-TS-84-202	2. Government Accession No.	3. Recipient's Catalog No.
4. Title and Subtitle Drainage of Highway Pavements		5. Report Date March 1984
		6. Performing Organization Code
7. Author(s) Frank L. Johnson and Fred F.M. Chang		8. Performing Organization Report No.
9. Performing Organization Name and Address Tye Engineering, Inc Centreville, Virginia 22020		10. Work Unit No. (TRAIS)
		11. Contract or Grant No.
		13. Type of Report and Period Covered
12. Sponsoring Agency Name and Address Federal Highway Administration Office of Implementation Engineering & Highway Operations McLean, Virginia 22101		
		14. Sponsoring Agency Code

15. Supplementary Notes
COTR: John M. Kurdziel
Technical Assistance: Stanley Davis, Daniel O'Connor, and Robert Baumgardner (HNG-31)

16. Abstract
This edition of Hydraulic Engineering Circular No. 12 incorporates new design charts and procedures developed from laboratory tests of interception capacities and efficiencies of highway pavement drainage inlets. A chart for the solution of the kinematic wave equation for overland flow and a new chart for the solution of Manning's equation for triangular channels are provided. Charts and procedures for using the charts are provided for 7 grate types, slotted drain inlets, curb-opening inlets, and combination inlets on grade and in sump locations. Charts, tables, and example problem solutions are included in the text where introduced and discussed.

The text includes discussion of the effects of roadway geometry on pavement drainage; the philosophy of design frequency and design spread selection; storm runoff estimating methods; flow in gutters; pavement drainage inlets, factors affecting capacity and efficiency, and comparisons of interception capacity; median inlets; embankment inlets; and bridge deck inlets. Five appendixes are included with discussion of the development of rainfall intensity-duration-frequency curves and equations, mean velocity in a reach of triangular channel with unsteady flow, the development of gutter capacity curves for compound and parabolic roadway sections, and the development of design charts for grates of specific size and bar configuration.

17. Key Words Pavement drainage inlets, inlet interception capacity, inlet efficiency, runoff, gutter flow spread, frontal flow, side flow bypass	18. Distribution Statement This document is available to the U.S. public through the National Technical Information Service, Springfield, Virginia 22161	
19. Security Classif. (of this report) Unclassified	20. Security Classif. (of this page) Unclassified	21. No. of Pages 151

22. Price

Form DOT F 1700.7 (8-72)   Reproduction of completed page authorized

Approximate Conversions from Metric Measures

LENGTH

Symbol	When You Know	Multiply by	To Find	Symbol
mm	millimeters	0.04	inches	in
cm	centimeters	0.4	inches	in
m	meters	3.3	feet	ft
m	meters	1.1	yards	yd
km	kilometers	0.6	miles	mi

AREA

Symbol	When You Know	Multiply by	To Find	Symbol
cm²	square centimeters	0.16	square inches	in²
m²	square meters	1.2	square yards	yd²
km²	square kilometers	0.4	square miles	mi²
ha	hectares (10,000 m²)	2.5	acres	

MASS (weight)

Symbol	When You Know	Multiply by	To Find	Symbol
g	grams	0.035	ounces	oz
kg	kilograms	2.2	pounds	lb
t	tonnes (1000 kg)	1.1	short tons	

VOLUME

Symbol	When You Know	Multiply by	To Find	Symbol
ml	milliliters	0.03	fluid ounces	fl oz
l	liters	2.1	pints	pt
l	liters	1.06	quarts	qt
l	liters	0.26	gallons	gal
m³	cubic meters	35	cubic feet	ft³
m³	cubic meters	1.3	cubic yards	yd³

TEMPERATURE (exact)

Symbol	When You Know	Multiply by	To Find	Symbol
°C	Celsius temperature	9/5 (then add 32)	Fahrenheit temperature	°F

°F
-40   0   32   80   98.6   120   160   200   212
-40   -20   0   20   37   40   60   80   100
°C

Approximate Conversions to Metric Measures

LENGTH

Symbol	When You Know	Multiply by	To Find	Symbol
in	inches	*2.5	centimeters	cm
ft	feet	30	centimeters	cm
yd	yards	0.9	meters	m
mi	miles	1.6	kilometers	km

AREA

Symbol	When You Know	Multiply by	To Find	Symbol
in²	square inches	6.5	square centimeters	cm²
ft²	square feet	0.09	square meters	m²
yd²	square yards	0.8	square meters	m²
mi²	square miles	2.6	square kilometers	km²
	acres	0.4	hectares	ha

MASS (weight)

Symbol	When You Know	Multiply by	To Find	Symbol
oz	ounces	28	grams	g
lb	pounds	0.45	kilograms	kg
	short tons (2000 lb)	0.9	tonnes	t

VOLUME

Symbol	When You Know	Multiply by	To Find	Symbol
tsp	teaspoons	5	milliliters	ml
Tbsp	tablespoons	15	milliliters	ml
fl oz	fluid ounces	30	milliliters	ml
c	cups	0.24	liters	l
pt	pints	0.47	liters	l
qt	quarts	0.95	liters	l
gal	gallons	3.8	liters	l
ft³	cubic feet	0.03	cubic meters	m³
yd³	cubic yards	0.76	cubic meters	m³

TEMPERATURE (exact)

Symbol	When You Know	Multiply by	To Find	Symbol
°F	Fahrenheit temperature	5/9 (after subtracting 32)	Celsius temperature	°C

*1 in = 2.54 (exactly). For other exact conversions and more detailed tables, see NBS Misc. Publ. 286, Units of Weights and Measures, Price $2.25, SD Catalog No. C13.10:286.

METRIC CONVERSION FACTORS

ii

TABLE OF CONTENTS

TABLE OF CONTENTS (Continued)

LIST OF FIGURES

LIST OF FIGURES (Continued)

LIST OF FIGURES (Continued)

LIST OF CHARTS

LIST OF TABLES

LIST OF SYMBOLS

a   Gutter depression, in (m).

A   Cross sectional area of flow, ft^2 (m^2);
Drainage area, acres (hectares);
The algebraic difference in approach gradients to a vertical curve, percent;
Orifice opening area, ft^2 (m^2).

B   Bottom width in a trapezoidal channel, ft (m);
Half-width of a parabolic street section, ft (m).

C   Rational equation coefficient of runoff.

C_o Orifice coefficient.

C_w Weir coefficient.

d   Depth of flow at the curb face, ft (m);
Depth of flow in an open channel, ft (m).

d_i Water depth at curb-opening lip, ft (m).

d_o Water depth to center of orifice opening, ft (m).

D   Diameter of a circular section, ft (m).

E   Interception efficiency of an inlet.

E_o Ratio of flow in a chosen width, usually the width of a grate, to total gutter flow.

g   Acceleration of gravity, ft/s/s (m/s/s).

h   Height of curb-opening orifice, ft (m).

H   Crown height on a parabolic street section, ft (m).

i   Rainfall intensity, in/hr (mm/hr).

K   Conveyance; the quantity flow rate divided by the square root of the longitudinal slope;
A constant describing the curvature of a vertical curve.

L   Overland flow length in the kinematic wave equation, ft (m);
Length of inlet, ft (m);
Vertical curve length, ft (m).

L_T Length of curb-opening or slotted drain inlet required for total gutter flow interception, ft (m).

n   Coefficient of roughness in Manning's equation.

P   Perimeter of a grate weir, ft (m).

Q   Flow rate; discharge, ft^3/s (m^3/s).

Q_b Bypass or carryover flow; the portion of total gutter flow which is not intercepted by an inlet, ft^3/s (m^3/s).

Q_i Intercepted flow; the portion of total gutter flow which is intercepted by an inlet, ft^3/s (m^3/s).

Q_s Side flow rate; flow rate outside of width, W, ft^3/s (m^3/s).

Q_w Flow rate in width, W, ft^3/s (m^3/s).

R_f Frontal flow interception efficiency for grates; the ratio of intercepted frontal flow to total frontal flow.

R_s Side flow interception efficiency for grates; the ratio of intercepted side flow to total side flow.

S   Slope of overland tributary area, ft/ft (m/m); Longitudinal slope of gutter or channel, ft/ft (m/m).

S_e Equivalent straight cross slope for a gutter section with a composite cross slope.

S_x Pavement cross slope, ft/ft (m/m)

S_w Cross slope of a depressed gutter, ft/ft (m/m).

S_w' Cross slope of a depressed gutter section measured from the normal cross slope of the pavement, ft/ft (m/m).

t_c Time of concentration for use in the Rational Method, min.

T   Spread of water on the pavement, ft (m).

T_a Spread where velocity is equal to average velocity in a reach of triangular gutter, ft (m)

V   Velocity, ft/s (m/s).

∇ Average velocity in a reach of gutter, ft/s (m/s)

V_o Velocity of flow at which splash-over first occurs over a grate, ft/s (m/s).

W   Width of a grate, ft (m);
Width of a depressed gutter, ft (m).

Z   Side slope ratio in a trapezoidal channel, horizontal to vertical.

GLOSSARY OF DESIGN TERMS

Bypass — Flow which bypasses an inlet on grade and is carried in the street or channel to the next inlet downgrade.

Carryover — See bypass.

Chute — A steep, inclined open channel (flume).

Combination Inlet — Drainage inlet usually composed of a curb-opening and a grate inlet.

Curb-opening Inlet — Drainage inlet consisting of an opening in the roadway curb.

Drop Inlet — Drainage inlet with a horizontal or nearly horizontal opening.

Equivalent cross slope — An imaginary straight cross slope having conveyance capacity equal to that of the given compound cross slope

Flanking Inlets — Inlets placed upstream and on either side of an inlet at the low point in a sag vertical curve. The purposes of these inlets are to intercept debris as the slope decreases and to act in relief of the inlet at the low point.

Frequency — Also referred to as exceedance interval, recurrence interval or return period; the average time interval between actual occurrences of a hydrological event of a given or greater magnitude; the reciprocal of the percent chance of occurrence in any one year period.

Frontal Flow — The portion of flow which passes over the upstream side of a grate.

Grate Inlet — Drainage inlet composed of a grate in the roadway section or at the roadside in a low point, swale or ditch.

Gutter	– That portion of the roadway section adjacent to the curb which utilized to convey storm runoff water. It may include a portion or all of a traveled lane, shoulder or parking lane, and a limited width adjacent to the curb may be of different materials and have a different cross slope.
Inlet Efficiency	– The ratio of flow intercepted by an inlet to total flow in the gutter.
Perimeter of a Grate	– The sum of the lengths of all sides of a grate, except that any side adjacent to a curb is not considered a part of the perimeter in weir flow computations.
Rainfall Intensity	– The average rate of rainfall for a selected time interval measured in inches/hour (m/h).
Runoff Coefficient	– As used in the Rational Method, the ratio of the rate of runoff to the rate of rainfall.
Scupper	– A vertical hole through a bridge deck for the purpose of deck drainage. Sometimes, a horizontal opening in the curb or barrier is called a scupper.
Side-flow Interception	– Flow which is intercepted along the side of a grate inlet, as opposed to frontal interception.
Slotted Drain Inlets	– Drainage inlet composed of a continuous slot built into the top of a pipe which serves to intercept, collect and transport the flow.
Splash-over	– Portion of the frontal flow at a grate which skips or splashes over the grate and is not intercepted.
Spread	– Width of flow measured laterally from the roadway curb.
Time of Concentration	– The time of flow from the hydraulically most distant point in the drainage area to the design point under consideration.

PRÈFACE

This second edition of Hydraulic Engineering Circular No. 12 incorporates new design charts and procedures to more clearly establish the interception capacity of roadway and median inlets. Design aids were developed from data from the several research reports cited in the text to apply to a wide range of design conditions.

Design charts are distinguished from figures used to illustrate text material by designating the curves to be used as design aids as Charts. Charts and tables are included in the text where introduced and discussed. Illustrative examples are provided to aid in understanding the use of the design aids, where appropriate.

Unit notations adopted for this publication are from the American Society of Testing Materials' "Standard for Metric Practice," ASTM Designation E 380-76. Quantities and values are expressed in English units throughout the text followed by the International System of Units (SI) equivalent in parenthesis. Metric conversion factors are furnished in the front material for conversion of English units used in figures, examples, and Charts.

U.S. DEPARTMENT OF TRANSPORTATION

FEDERAL HIGHWAY ADMINISTRATION

DRAINAGE OF HIGHWAY PAVEMENTS

1.0 INTRODUCTION

Effective drainage of highway pavements is essential to maintenance of the service level of highways and to traffic safety. Water on the pavement slows traffic and contributes to accidents from hydroplaning and loss of visibility from splash and spray. Free-standing puddles which engage only one side of a vehicle are perhaps the most hazardous because of the dangerous

torque levels exerted on the vehicle (1)[1]. Thus, the design of the surface drainage system is particularly important at locations where ponding can occur.

Discussion in this Circular is limited to the subject of the removal of storm water from highway pavement surfaces and median areas. It does not include the conveyance systems which carry the water from the inlet to the point of discharge. Information on highway geometric design is taken from American Association of State Highway and Transportation Officials (AASHTO) policy (2). Design charts were developed from data from comprehensive research on drainage inlet interception sponsored by the Federal Highway Administration at the Bureau of Reclamation hydraulics laboratory (3-7).

In this Circular, roadway geometry as it affects pavement drainage is discussed first. Estimating storm water runoff for inlet design is next discussed and then flow in curbed gutter sections. Discussions of types of inlets, factors affecting inlet interception capacity, inlet interception capacity comparisons, and design charts are included in sections 6 through 8. Median, embankment and bridge inlets are discussed in section 10. Finally, procedures for developing design charts for parabolic roadway sections and for standard inlet configurations and cross slopes used by a highway design agency, rainfall intensity curves and equations, and the derivation of the equation for mean velocity in a gutter section are provided in appendixes.

---

1. Underlined numbers in parenthesis refer to publications listed in the references in section 11.0.

2.0 ROADWAY GEOMETRY

Roadway design geometric features greatly influence the
feasibility of providing for satisfactory drainage of highway
pavement surfaces. These features include curbs, gutter configuration, longitudinal and lateral pavement slopes, shoulders, and
parking lanes. The effects of these geometric features on highway pavement drainage are discussed in the following sections.

2.1 Longitudinal Grades

It is more important to maintain a minimum longitudinal
gradient on curbed pavements than on uncurbed pavements in order
to avoid undue spread of storm water on the pavement. However,
flat gradients on uncurbed pavements introduce the problem of
spread on the pavement where vegetation builds up along the
pavement edge. It may also be difficult to maintain sufficient
fall in roadside channels to drain cut sections and medians
adequately where near-zero pavement gradients are used.

Gutter grades should not be less than 0.3 percent for curbed
pavements, and not less than 0.2 percent in very flat terrain.
Minimum grades can be maintained in very flat terrain by use of a
rolling profile or by warping the cross slope to achieve a
rolling gutter profile.

To provide adequate drainage in sag vertical curves, a
minimum slope of 0.3 percent should be maintained within 50 ft
(15.2 m) of the level point in the curve. (As used in this
Circular, sag vertical curves are only those between negative and
positive grades. Curves between two positive grades or two
negative grades are excluded.) This is accomplished where the
length of the curve, L, divided by the algebraic difference in
grades, A, is equal to or less than 167 (L/A $\leq$ 167). Although
ponding is not usually a problem at crest vertical curves, a
similar minimum gradient should be provided to facilitate drainage.

2.2 Cross Slopes

Pavement cross slope is often a compromise between the need
for reasonably steep cross slopes for drainage and relatively
flat cross slopes for driver comfort. It has been found ([1]) that
cross slopes of 2 percent have little effect on driver effort in
steering, especially with power steering, or on friction demand
for vehicle stability.

2

Water on the pavement is the principal cause of loss of tire contact with the pavement in hydroplaning incidents. Horizontal drag forces are imposed on the vehicle by the water, and, if the forces are unevenly distributed laterally, e.g., by ponding against a curb, can cause hazardous directional instability (1). Water depth on the pavement varies with pavement texture, length of the flow path, rainfall intensity, and inversely with the slope of the drainage path. The length of the flow path is decreased and the slope increased with steeper cross slopes. Therefore, adequate cross slope is a highly important counter-measure against hydroplaning. An increase in cross slope for each successive lane of multilane facilities is an effective measure in reducing water depth on pavements. Where practicable, inside lanes can be sloped toward the median; median areas should not be drained across traveled lanes. A careful check should be made of designs to minimize the number and length of flat pavement sections in cross slope transition areas, and consideration should be given to increasing cross slopes in sag vertical curves, crest vertical curves, and in sections of flat longitudinal grades. Where curbs are used, depressed gutter sections should be considered as an effective measure for increasing gutter capacity and reducing spread on the pavement.

Shoulders are generally sloped to drain away from the pavement, except with raised, narrow medians. Crossover from superelevated curves to shoulders is limited to 8 percent.

Table 1 shows the range in rates of cross slope for various conditions (2).

2.3 Curb and Gutter Design

A complete discussion of the geometrics of curbs and gutters is beyond the scope of this Circular and discussion here is limited to the effects of curbs and gutters on the drainage of highway pavements.

Curbing at the right edge of pavements is normal practice for low-speed, urban highway facilities. Gutters may be 1 to 6 feet wide but are usually confined to a width of 1 to 3 feet adjacent to the curb. Gutter cross slopes may be the same as that of the pavement, or gutters may be designed with a steeper cross slope, usually 1 inch per foot (0.083 m/m) steeper than the pavement. Curbs should be at the outside edge of shoulders or parking lanes, if used. The gutter pan width may be included as a part of the parking lane.

Table 1. Normal pavement cross slopes.

	Range in Rate of Cross Slope
High-type Surface 2 - lanes 3 or more lanes in each direction	0.015 - 0.020 0.015 minimum; increase 0.005 - 0.010/lane 0.040 maximum
Intermediate surface	0.015 - 0.030
Low-type surface	0.020 - 0.060
Urban Arterials	0.015 - 0.030; increase 0.010/lane
Shoulders Bituminous or Concrete With Curbs	0.02 - 0.06 $\geq$ 0.04

Notes: (1) With curbs, the lower values above are questionable.
(2) With steeper gutters, lesser rates of cross slope are permissible.

Where practicable, it is desirable to intercept runoff from cut slopes and other areas draining toward the roadway before it reaches the highway, in order to minimize the deposition of sediment and other debris on the roadway and to reduce the amount of water which must be carried in the gutter section.

Shallow swale sections at the edge of the roadway pavement or shoulder offer advantages over curbed sections where curbs are not needed for traffic control. These advantages include a lesser hazard to traffic than a near-vertical curb and hydraulic capacity that is not dependent on spread on the pavement. Swale sections are particularly appropriate where curbs are generally used to prevent water from eroding fill slopes.

2.4 Roadside and Median Ditches

Medians are commonly used to separate opposing lanes of traffic on divided highways. On undivided, multilane facilities, median areas may be used as turning lanes or paint stripes may be

4

used to control indiscriminate left turns. Where practicable, it is preferable to slope median areas and inside shoulders to a center swale to prevent drainage from the median area from running across the pavement. This is particularly important for high-speed facilities, for facilities with more than two lanes of traffic in each direction, and where snow melt from median areas would flow across traffic lanes.

Roadside ditches are commonly used with uncurbed roadway sections to convey runoff from the highway pavement and areas which drain toward the highway. Roadside ditches can not be used on many urban arterials but can be used in cut sections, depressed sections, and other locations where driveways and intersections are infrequent. Curbed highway sections are relatively inefficient in conveying water, and the area tributary to the gutter section should be kept to a minimum in order to minimize the hazard from water on the pavement. Where practicable, it is desirable to intercept flow from all areas draining toward curbed highway pavements.

2.5 Bridge Decks

Effective bridge deck drainage is important for several reasons including the susceptibility of the deck structural and reinforcing steel to corrosion from deicing salts, ice forming on bridge decks while other roadway surfaces are still ice-free, and the possibility of hydroplaning on decks with little surface texture. While bridge deck drainage is accomplished in the same manner as drainage of other curbed roadway sections, they are often less effectively drained because of lower cross slopes, uniform cross slopes for traffic lanes and shoulders, parapets which collect relatively large amounts of debris, drainage inlets which are relatively small, and clogging of inlets and drainage systems.

Because of the difficulties in providing for adequate deck drainage and in providing for adequate maintenance of deck drainage systems, gutter flow from roadways should be intercepted before it reaches a bridge. Where practicable, all deck drainage should be carried to the bridge end for disposal. For similar reasons, zero gradients and sag vertical curves should be avoided on bridges.

3.0 DESIGN FREQUENCY AND SPREAD

Two of the more significant variables considered in the design of highway pavement drainage are the frequency of the runoff event for design and the spread of water on the pavement during the design event. A related consideration is the use of an event of lesser frequency to check the drainage design.

Spread and design frequency are not independent. The implications of the use of a criteria for spread of one-half of a traffic lane is considerably different for one design frequency than for a lesser frequency. It also has different implications for a low-traffic, low-speed highway than for a higher classification highway. These subjects are central to the issue of highway pavement drainage and important to highway safety.

3.1 Selection of Design Frequency and Design Spread

The objective in the design of a drainage system for a curbed highway pavement section is to collect runoff in the gutter and convey it to pavement inlets in a manner that provides reasonable safety for traffic and pedestrians at a reasonable cost. As spread from the curb increases, the risks of traffic accidents and delays and the nuisance and possible hazard to pedestrian traffic increase.

The process of selecting the recurrence interval and spread for design involves decisions regarding acceptable risks of accidents and traffic delays and acceptable costs for the drainage system. Risks associated with water on traffic lanes are greater with high traffic volumes, high speeds, and higher highway classifications than with lower volumes, speeds, and highway classification.

Following is a summary of the major considerations that enter into the selection of design frequency and design spread.

1. The classification of the highway is a good starting point in the selection process since it defines the public's expectations regarding water on the pavement surface. Ponding on traffic lanes of high-speed, high-volume highways is contrary to the public's expectations and thus the risks of accidents and the costs of traffic delays are high.

2. Design speed is important to the selection of design criteria. At speeds greater than 45 mi/hr (72 km/hr), water on the pavement can cause hydroplaning.

6

Figure 1. Spread greater than "allowable" on a major arterial.

3. Projected traffic volumes are an indicator of the economic
    importance of keeping the highway open to traffic. The
    costs of traffic delays and accidents increase with increas-
    ing traffic volumes.

4. The intensity of rainfall events may significantly affect
    the selection of design frequency and spread. Risks asso-
    ciated with the spread of water on pavements may be less in
    arid areas subject to high intensity thunderstorm events
    than in areas accustomed to frequent but less intense
    events.

5. Capital costs are neither the least nor last consideration.
    Cost considerations make it necessary to formulate a ration-
    al approach to the selection of design criteria. "Trade-
    offs" between desirable and practicable criteria are some-
    times necessary because of costs. In particular, the costs
    and feasibility of providing for a given design frequency
    and spread may vary significantly between projects. In some
    cases, it may be practicable to significantly upgrade the
    drainage design and reduce risks at moderate costs. In
    other instances, as where extensive outfalls or pumping

stations are required, costs may be very sensitive to the criteria selected for use in design.

Other considerations include inconvenience, hazards and nuisances to pedestrian traffic. These considerations should not be minimized and, in some locations such as in commercial areas, may assume major importance. Local design practice may also be a major consideration since it can affect the feasibility of designing to higher standards, and it influences the public's perception of acceptable practice.

The relative elevation of the highway and surrounding terrain is an additional consideration where water can be drained only through a storm drainage system, as in underpasses and depressed sections. The potential for ponding to hazardous depths should be considered in selecting the frequency and spread criteria and in checking the design against storm runoff events of lesser frequency than the design event.

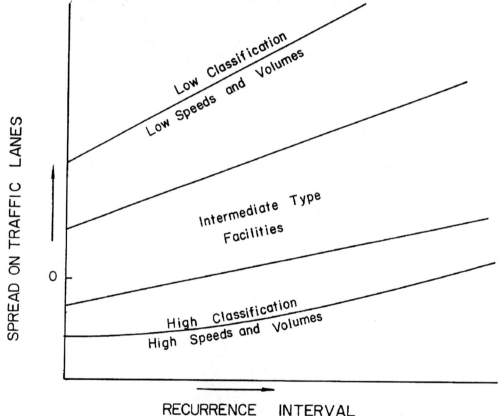

Figure 2. Design spread vs. design recurrence interval.

Figure 2 shows the interrelationship of highway classification, traffic volumes and speeds, and design frequency and
spread. The purpose of the figure is to illustrate that as the
risks associated with water on traffic lanes increase with
increasing speeds and traffic volumes, and higher highway classifications, the need to design for lesser spread on the pavement
and lesser frequency storm events also increases. A multi-
dimensional matrix or figure would be required to represent all
of the considerations involved in selecting design criteria;
however, figure 2 can be taken to present some of the factors
which enter into decisionmaking. The figure illustrates that
high speed, high volume facilities, such as freeways, should be
designed to minimize or eliminate spread on the traffic lanes
during the design event. A relatively low recurrence interval,
such as a 10-year frequency, is commonly used and spread can
usually be limited to shoulders.

Spread on traffic lanes can be tolerated more frequently and
to greater widths where traffic volumes and speeds are low. A 2-
year recurrence interval and corresponding spreads of one-half of
a traffic lane or more are usually considered a minimum type
design for low-volume local roads.

The selection of design criteria for intermediate types of
facilities may be the most difficult. For example, some arterials with relatively high traffic volumes and speeds may not have
shoulders which will convey the design runoff without encroaching
on the traffic lanes. In these instances, an assessment of the
relative risks and costs of various design spreads may be helpful
in selecting appropriate design criteria.

3.2 Selection of Check Storm and Spread

The design frequency usually used in the design of depressed
sections and underpasses is greatly influenced by Federal Highway
Administration policy which has required the use of a 50-year
frequency for underpasses and depressed sections on Interstate
highways where ponded water can be removed only through the storm
drain system. This policy has also been widely used at similar
locations for other highways. The use of a lesser frequency
event, such as a 50-year storm, to assess hazards at critical
locations where water can pond to appreciable depths is commonly
referred to as a check storm or check event.

The use of a check event is considered advisable if a
sizeable area which drains to the highway could cause unaccept-
able flooding during events that exceed the design event. Also,
the design of any series of inlets should be checked against a

9

larger runoff event where the series terminates at a sag vertical curve in which ponding to hazardous depths could occur.

The frequency selected for use as the check storm should be based on the same considerations used to select the design storm, i.e., the consequences of spread exceeding that chosen for design and the potential for ponding. Where no significant ponding can occur, check storms are normally unnecessary. Where significant ponding can occur in the area of Federal Emergency Management Agency-insured buildings, a 100-year recurrence interval storm should be used for the check storm if the ponding could cause the buildings to flood.

A criteria for spread during the check event is also desirable. Two criteria which have been used are: one lane open to traffic during the check storm event, and one lane free of water during the check storm event. These criteria differ sub-stantively, but each sets a standard by which the design can be evaluated.

4.0 ESTIMATING STORM RUNOFF

Areas contributing storm runoff to highway pavement drainage inlets are usually small in size. Curbed highway pavements are not designed to convey large discharges and water on the traffic lanes impedes traffic and impairs highway safety. It has been considered good practice, therefore, to intercept flow from drainage areas of substantial size before it reaches the highway.

The most commonly used method for estimating runoff for highway pavement drainage is the Rational Method. In recent years, however, digital computers have made it possible to use more sophisticated methods. In general, the methods are much too complex, take more computer time than is warranted for the design of pavement drainage, and the improvement in accuracy is problematical (8).

4.1 Rational Method

The Rational Method was first referred to in American literature in 1889 by Kuichling (9). The Rational formula is:

$$Q = KCiA \tag{1}$$

where: Q = the peak runoff rate, ft^3/s (m^3/s)
K = 1 (0.00275)
C = a dimensionless runoff coefficient representing characteristics of the watershed
i = the average rainfall intensity, in/hr (mm/hr) for a duration equal to the time of concentration and for the recurrence interval recurrence chosen for design
A = drainage area, acres (hectares) (10).

Assumptions implicit in the Rational Method are (9, 11):

1. The rate of runoff resulting from any rainfall intensity is greatest when the rainfall intensity lasts as long or longer than the time of concentration.

2. The probability of exceedance of the peak runoff rate as computed is the same as the probability of the average rainfall intensity used in the method.

3. A straight-line relationship exists between the maximum rate of runoff and a rainfall intensity of duration equal to or longer than the time of concentration, e.g., a

2-inch/hour (5 mm/hr) rainfall will result in a peak discharge exactly twice as large as a 1-inch/hour (2.5 mm/hr) average intensity rainfall.

4. The coefficient of runoff is the same for storms of all recurrence probabilities.

5. The coefficient of runoff is the same for all storms on a given watershed.

Use of the Rational Method is described in references (10), (12), and elsewhere in the literature.

4.1.1 Coefficient of Runoff

The runoff coefficient, C, characterizes antecedent precipitation, soil moisture, infiltration, detention, ground slope, ground cover, evaporation, shape of the watershed and other variables. Various adjustments to the coefficient have been suggested (10, 12) to account for variability due to prior wetting and storm duration. For relatively small watersheds such as those dealt with in the surface drainage of highway pavements, adjustments are probably unwarranted. Average values for various surface types, which are assumed not to vary during the storm, are commonly used. Values of C are given in table 2.

Table 2. Values of runoff coefficient, C, for use in the Rational Equation

Type of Surface	Runoff Coefficient, C
Paved	0.7 - 0.9
Gravel roadways or shoulders	0.4 - 0.6
Cut, fill slopes	0.5 - 0.7
Grassed areas	0.1 - 0.7
Residential	0.3 - 0.7
Woods	0.1 - 0.3
Cultivated	0.2 - 0.6

Note: For flat slopes and permeable soils, use the lower values. For steep slopes and impermeable soils, use the higher values. See reference (12) for a detailed list of coefficients currently in use.

Where drainage areas are composed of parts having different runoff characteristics, a weighted coefficient for the total drainage area is computed by dividing the summation of the products of the area of the parts and their coefficients by the total area, i.e.,

$$C_w = \frac{C_1 A_1 + C_2 A_2 + \cdots + C_n A_n}{A_t}$$

4.1.2 Rainfall Intensity

It is necessary to have information on the intensity, duration, and frequency of rainfall for the locality of the design in order to make use of the Rational Method.

Precipitation intensity-duration-frequency (I-D-F) curves can be developed from information in the following National Weather Service publications:

NOAA Technical Memorandum NWS HYDRO-35, "5 to 60 - Minute Precipitation Frequency for Eastern and Central United States," 1977.

NOAA Atlas 2. Precipitation Atlas of the Western United States, 1973.
Vol. I, Montana   Vol. II, Wyoming   Vol. III, Colorado
Vol. IV, New Mexico   Vol. V, Idaho   Vol. VI, Utah
Vol. VII, Nevada   Vol. VIII, Arizona   Vol. IX, Washington
Vol. X, Oregon   Vol. XI, California
Technical Paper 42, Puerto Rico and Virgin Islands, 1961
Technical Paper 43, Hawaii, 1962
Technical Paper 47, Alaska, 1963

HYDRO-35 contains precipitation and frequency information for durations of 60 minutes and less for the 37 States from North Dakota to Texas and eastward. For durations greater than 60 minutes, the following publication is applicable for the above States:

Technical Paper No. 40. 48 contiguous states, 1961.

The greatest differences between HYDRO-35 and TP-40 are in the 5-min map in which values differ substantially in Maine, parts of the northern plains, along the Gulf Coast, and along the Atlantic Coast.

Maps from HYDRO-35, an example development of an I-D-F curve and a procedure for developing precipitation intensity-duration equations are included in Appendix A.

The 11 volumes of NOAA Atlas 2 replace TP-40 for the eleven western conterminous States. Investigations for the Atlas were undertaken to depict more accurately variations in the precipitation - frequency regime in mountainous regions.

It is impractical to include maps from the 11 volumes of NOAA Atlas 2 in this Circular because of the number and size of the maps. Differences in values from TP-40, particularly in areas of orographic influences on precipitation, make it advisable for agencies to develop new I-D-F curves based on information taken from the Atlas. An example development of an I-D-F curve and equations for the curves are included in Appendix A.

4.1.3 Time of Concentration

Time of concentration is defined as the time it takes for runoff to travel from the hydraulically most distant point in the watershed to the point of reference downstream. An assumption implicit to the Rational Method is that the peak runoff rate occurs when the rainfall intensity lasts as long or longer than the time of concentration. Therefore, the time of concentration for the drainage area must be estimated in order to select the appropriate value of rainfall intensity for use in the equation.

The time of concentration for inlets is comprised of at least two components. These are overland flow time and gutter flow time. If overland flow is channelized upstream of the location at which the flow enters the highway gutter, a third component is added.

A thorough study at the University of Maryland (13) found that the most realistic method for estimating overland flow time of concentration was the kinematic wave equation:

$$t_c = \frac{K\ L^{0.6} n^{0.6}}{i^{0.4} S^{0.3}} \tag{2}$$

where: t_c = the time of overland flow in seconds
   L = overland flow length, ft (m)
   n = Manning roughness coefficient
   i = rainfall rate, in/hr (m/hr)
   S = the average slope of the overland area
   K = 56 (26.285)

Chart 1 is a nomograph for the solution of the kinematic wave equation for overland flow.

The kinematic wave theory is consistent with the latest concepts of fluid mechanics and considers all those parameters found important in overland flow when the flow is turbulent (where the product of the rainfall intensity and length of the slope is in excess of 500).

When using the nomograph, Manning roughness coefficients of 0.013 for concrete and 0.50 for turf were recommended. Since these values are in close agreement with normal flow data, Manning coefficients obtained from flow experiments on other surfaces are satisfactory for use.

In using the nomograph, the time of concentration and rainfall intensity are unknown. The solution is one of iteration or trial and error. A value for i is first assumed and the related time of concentration is read from Chart 1. The assumed rainfall intensity must then be checked against the I-D-F curve for the frequency of the event chosen for the particular design problem, and the procedure repeated until the assumed rainfall intensity is in agreement with the intensity associated with the time of concentration. Example 1 illustrates the procedure.

Example 1:

Given: L = 150 ft
        S = 0.02
        n = 0.4 (turf)
        Design frequency - 10 yr
        Location: Colorado Springs, Colorado

Find: Overland flow time, t_c

Solution:
        (1) Assume i = 5 in/hr
            t_c = 23 min (Chart 1)
            i = 3.3 in/hr (figure 29)

        (2) Try i = 3.5 in/hr
            t_c = 20 min (Chart 1)
            i = 3.6 in/hr (figure 29)

Since the trial rainfall intensity is in close agreement with the intensity read from figure 29, the time of concentration for overland flow is 20 min. Use of Chart 1 in this example requires that the second turning line be extended. A folded arrangement of the turning lines would eliminate the

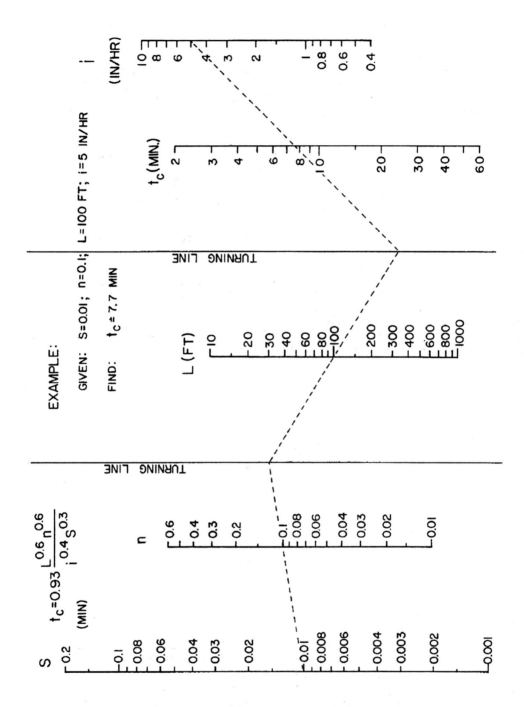

CHART 1. Kinematic wave formulation for determining time of concentration.

need to extend the turning lines, but Chart 1 was adopted because use of a folded scale is more complicated.

In order to find the time of flow in the gutter flow component of the time of concentration, a method for estimating the average velocity in a reach of gutter is needed. The time of flow in a triangular channel with uniform inflow per unit of length can be accurately estimated by use of an average velocity of flow in the gutter. Integration of the Manning equation for a right triangular channel with respect to time and distance yields an average velocity for the channel length at the point where spread is equal to 65 percent of the maximum spread for channels with zero flow at the upstream end. For channel sections with flow rates greater than zero at the upstream end, as with carryover from an inlet, the spread at average velocity (T_a) is given by table 3 (See figure 38, Appendix B). In table 3, T_1 is

spread at the upstream end and T_2 is spread at the downstream end

of the reach of gutter under consideration. Chart 2 is a nomograph to solve for velocity in a triangular channel with known cross slope, slope and spread. Example 2 illustrates the use of Chart 2 and table 3.

Table 3. Spread at average velocity in a reach of triangular gutter.

T_1/T_2	0	0.1	0.2	0.3	0.4	0.5	0.6	0.7	0.8
T_a/T_2	0.65	0.66	0.68	0.70	0.74	0.77	0.82	0.86	0.90

Example 2:

Given: T_1 = 4 ft (bypass flow from inlet upstream)
         T_2 = 10 ft (design spread at second inlet)
         S = 0.03
         S_x = 0.02
         Inlet Spacing = 300 ft (estimated)

Find: Time of flow in gutter

Solution:
         T_1/T_2 = 0.4
         T_a/T_2 = 0.74 (table 3)
         T_a = 10 x 0.74 = 7.4 ft
         V_a = 3.5 ft/s (Chart 2)
         t_a = 300/3.5 = 86 sec = 1.4 min

17

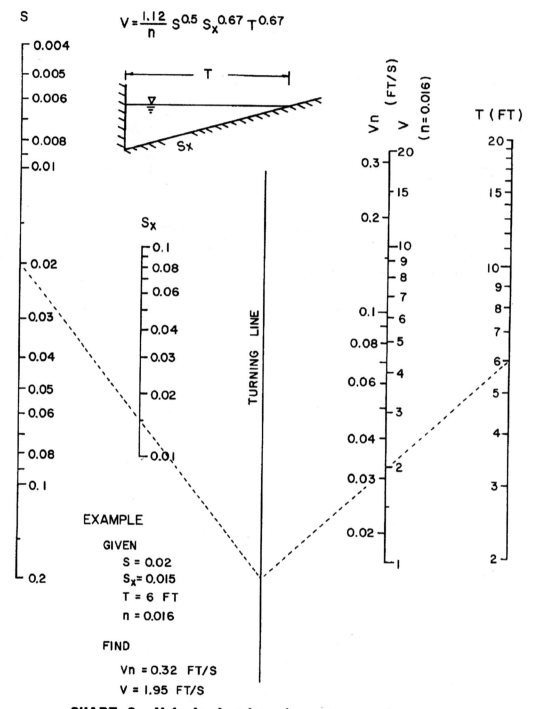

CHART 2. Velocity in triangular gutter sections.

In practice, the two components of the time of concentration are added to get the total time. For the examples here, the time of concentration is 20 + 2 = 22 minutes.

The time of concentration for a drainage area composed entirely of highway pavement is estimated in the same manner as in the above examples. Because of the short distance of overland flow, the total time of concentration for pavement drainage inlets will be less than 5 minutes at most locations where the drainage area is highway pavement.

Where overland flow becomes channelized upstream of the highway pavement, it is usually good practice to intercept the flow before it reaches the highway gutter. Interception may be by a cross drainage structure, a roadside ditch, or a roadside inlet. The time of concentration for such a drainage area is computed by adding the time of overland flow from the hydraulically most distant point in the drainage area to the time of flow in the channel from the point at which overland flow enters the channel. Chart 1 can be used as illustrated to compute the overland flow time component of the time of concentration. Any of many design aids available may be used to compute channel flow time. Chart 16, section 10.1, is an example of the design aids which can be used to compute flow depth in a channel. From flow depth, the cross sectional area of flow can be computed and velocity can be computed by use of the continuity equation:

$$Q = AV \qquad\qquad (3)$$

where: A = cross sectional area of flow, ft^2 (m^2)
   V = velocity of flow, ft/s (m/s)

4.1.4 Computing Runoff

Runoff from a drainage area consisting of only one surface drainage type is computed as illustrated by the following example:

Example 3:

Given: A highway in Charlotte, NC; a 32 ft width of pavement
   drains toward the gutter
   $S = 0.005$
   $S_x = 0.03$
   $n = 0.016$
   $T = 8$ ft (width of parking lane)
   $S_x = 0.05$ (parking lane)
   $C = 0.9$

19

```
      Design frequency = 10 yr
      t_c = 5 min
```

Find: Rainfall intensity and runoff from 500 ft of pavement

Solution:
```
      i = 7.2 in/hr (figure 34)
      Q = CiA = 0.9 x 7.2 x (32 x 500)/43,560 = 2.4 ft^3/s
```

Computing the runoff from a non-homogeneous area is general-ly accomplished by using a weighted coefficient for the total area and rainfall intensity corresponding to the longest time of concentration to the point for which the runoff is to be determined. On some combinations of drainage areas, it is poss-ible that the maximum rate of runoff will occur from the higher intensity rainfall for periods less than the time of concentra-tion for the total area, even though only a part of the drainage area may be contributing. This might occur where a part of the drainage area is highly impervious and has a short time of concentration, and another part is pervious and has a much longer time of concentration. Unless the areas or times of concentra-tion are considerably out of balance, however, the range of accuracy of the method does not warrant checking the peak flow from only a part of the drainage area. For the relatively small drainage areas associated with highway pavement drainage, it can usually be assumed that the longest time of concentration for the drainage area is appropriate for purposes of computing runoff.

4.2 Other Runoff Estimating Methods

Numerous runoff simulation models have been developed in recent years because of the interest in stormwater management for pollution and flood abatement. The more recent models require the use of high-speed computers and output runoff hydrographs from inputs of rainfall hyetographs and drainage basin data on infiltration, land use, antecedent rainfall, and other physical data. Insofar as the mainframe computer programs developed to date are concerned, they are useful for flood routing and flood storage planning, but because of the approximations used for inlet interception, they are not particularly useful for pavement drainage design.

Other runoff estimating methods which do not require the use of computers are also available, including the British Road Research Laboratory method (TRRL), the unit hydrograph method, and the Soil Conservation Service methods. The unit hydrograph method requires rainfall and runoff data to develop the unit graph and has little applicability to pavement inlet design.

The TRRL method can be used to estimate peak flow rates. The method considers only the directly connected impervious areas, i.e., impervious areas that drain to an intermediate area that is pervious prior to interception are not considered. The method requires a design hyetograph and mapping of isocrones, or lines of equal time of travel to the catchment outlet. Runoff computations are based on 100 percent runoff from impervious areas from rainfall intensity increments corresponding to the time interval between isocrones (11).

The TRRL has little applicability to highway pavement drainage because inlet time is usually too short to develop isocrones for the drainage area, pervious areas are neglected, and a rainfall hyetograph is required. Where other impervious areas are combined with highway pavement drainage, the method could be used.

The Soil Conservation Service (SCS) method in Technical Release 55 (TR-55) is based on numerous computer runs using the SCS continuous simulation model, TR-20. It is applicable to watersheds of 1 to 2,000 acres (0.4 to 809 hectares) and provides a means for estimating peak discharge. The method has application where design for storage is necessary but has little application for pavement inlet design. The method can be used for drainage areas which include areas outside the highway pavement, as for roadside ditches and drainage systems which combine highway pavement drainage with other drainage. Application of the method requires identification of hydrologic soil groups, watershed area, percent impervious, and overall slope. The 24-hour rainfall volume for the design recurrence interval is selected from the SCS Type II Rainfall Hyetograph and runoff volume is determined from a table using runoff curve numbers and rainfall volume. Runoff volume is then converted to peak discharge by use of a multiplier obtained from charts relating curve number and slope to drainage area and peak discharge. Further adjustments can then be made for the effects of imperviousness if the user is not convinced that all effects of imperviousness are accounted for in the selection of the runoff curve number (11).

5.0 FLOW IN GUTTERS

A pavement gutter is defined, for purposes of this Circular, as the section of pavement next to the curb which conveys water during a storm runoff event. It may include a portion or all of a travel lane. Gutter cross sections usually have a triangular shape with the curb forming the near-vertical leg of the triangle. The gutter may have a straight cross slope or a cross slope composed of two straight lines. Parabolic sections are also used, especially on older pavements and on city streets.

Modification of the Manning equation is necessary for use in computing flow in triangular channels because the hydraulic radius in the equation does not adequately describe the gutter cross section, particularly where the top width of the water surface may be more than 40 times the depth at the curb. To compute gutter flow, the Manning equation is integrated for an increment of width across the section (14). The resulting equation in terms of cross slope and spread on the pavement is:

$$Q = (K/n) S_x^{5/3} S^{1/2} T^{8/3} \tag{4}$$

where: $K = 0.56 \ (0.016)$
Q = flow rate ft^3/s (m^3/s)
T = width of flow (spread), ft (m)
S_x = cross slope, ft/ft (m/m)
S = longitudinal slope, ft/ft (m/m)

Equation (4) neglects the resistance of the curb face, but this resistance is negligible from a practical point of view if the cross slope is 10 percent or less.

Spread on the pavement and flow depth at the curb are often used as criteria for spacing pavement drainage inlets. Chart 3 is a nomograph for solving equation (4). The Chart can be used for either criterion with the relationship:

$$d = T S_x \tag{5}$$

Chart 3 can be used for direct solution of gutter flow where the Manning n value is 0.016. For other values of n, divide the value of Qn by n. Instructions for use and an example problem solution are provided on the Chart.

5.1 Gutters of Uniform Cross Slope

The use of Chart 3 to compute flow in a gutter of uniform

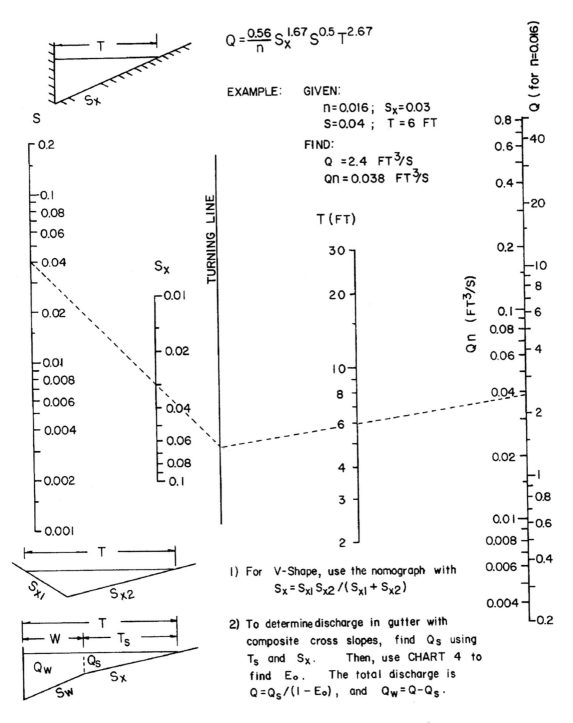

$$Q = \frac{0.56}{n} S_x^{1.67} S^{0.5} T^{2.67}$$

EXAMPLE: GIVEN:
  $n = 0.016$; $S_x = 0.03$
  $S = 0.04$; $T = 6$ FT

FIND:
  $Q = 2.4$ FT^3/S
  $Qn = 0.038$ FT^3/S

1) For V-Shape, use the nomograph with
   $S_x = S_{x1} S_{x2} / (S_{x1} + S_{x2})$

2) To determine discharge in gutter with
   composite cross slopes, find Q_s using
   T_s and S_x.   Then, use CHART 4 to
   find E_o.   The total discharge is
   $Q = Q_s / (1 - E_o)$, and $Q_w = Q - Q_s$.

CHART 3. Flow in triangular gutter sections.

23

cross slope is illustrated in example 4.

Example 4:

Given: T = 8 ft
         S_x = 0.025
         S = 0.01
         n = 0.015
         d = TS_x = 8 x 0.025 = 0.2 ft

Find: (1) Flow in gutter at design spread
         (2) Flow in width W = 2 ft adjacent to the curb

Solution:
         (1) From Chart 3, Qn = 0.03
             Q = Qn/n = 0.03/0.015 = 2.0 ft^3/s

         (2) T = 8 - 2 = 6 ft
             $(Qn)_2$ = 0.014 (Chart 3) (flow in 6 ft width outside
                             of width W)

             Q = 0.014/0.015 = 0.9 ft^3/s

             Q_w = 2.0 - 0.9 = 1.1 ft^3/s

Flow in the first 2 ft adjacent to the curb is 1.1 ft^3/s and

0.9 ft^3/s in the remainder of the gutter.

5.2 Composite Gutter Sections

Chart 4 is provided for use with Chart 3 to find the flow in
a width of gutter, W, less than total spread, T. It can be used
for either a straight cross slope or a composite gutter slope.
The procedure for use of the Chart is illustrated in example 5.

Example 5:

Given: T = 8 ft
         S_x = 0.025

         Gutter depression = 2 in = 0.167 ft
         W = 2 ft
         S_w = (0.167/2) + 0.025 = 0.108
         S = 0.01
         n = 0.015
         d = TS_x + 2/12 = 8 x 0.025 + 0.17 = 0.37 ft

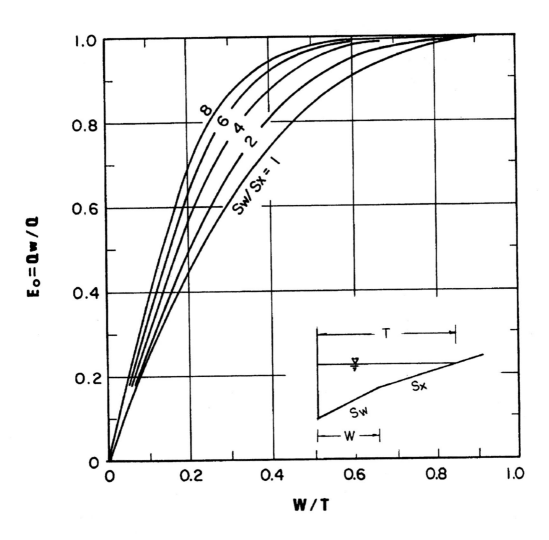

CHART 4. Ratio of frontal flow to total gutter flow.

25

Find: (1) Total gutter flow
      (2) Flow in the 2 ft depressed section

Solution:
$$T - W = 8 - 2 = 6 \text{ ft}$$
$$Q_s n = 0.14 \quad \text{(Flow in 6 ft section) (Chart 3)}$$

$$Q_s = Q_s n/n = 0.014/0.015 = 0.9 \text{ ft}^3/\text{s}$$

$$W/T = 2/8 = 0.25$$

$$\frac{S_w}{S_x} = \frac{0.108}{0.025} = 4.32$$

$$E_o = 0.69 \quad \text{(Chart 4)}$$

(1) Total flow in the gutter section:
$$Q = Q_s/(1 - E_o) = 0.9/(1 - 0.69) = 3.0 \text{ ft}^3/\text{s}$$

(2) Flow in the 2 ft width, W:
$$Q_w = Q - Q_s = 3.0 - 0.9 = 2.1 \text{ ft}^3/\text{s}$$

Chart 5 provides for a direct solution of gutter flow in a composite gutter section. The flow rate at a given spread or the spread at a known flow rate can be found from the Chart.

Chart 5 is an exact solution of the equation for flow in a composite gutter section, but the nature of the equation requires a complex graphical solution. Typical of graphical solutions such as this, extreme care in using the Chart is necessary to obtain accurate results. An alternative to Chart 5 is a series of charts such as that illustrated in figure 3. A chart for each depressed gutter configuration is necessary, and it is impractical to include all possible configurations in this Circular. The procedure for developing charts for depressed gutter conveyance is included as Appendix C.

5.3 Gutters with Curved Cross Sections

Where the pavement cross section is curved, gutter capacity varies with the configuration of the pavement. For this reason, discharge-spread or discharge-depth-at-the-curb relationships developed for one pavement configuration are not applicable to another section with a different crown height or half-width.

Procedures for developing conveyance curves for parabolic pavement sections are included in Appendix D.

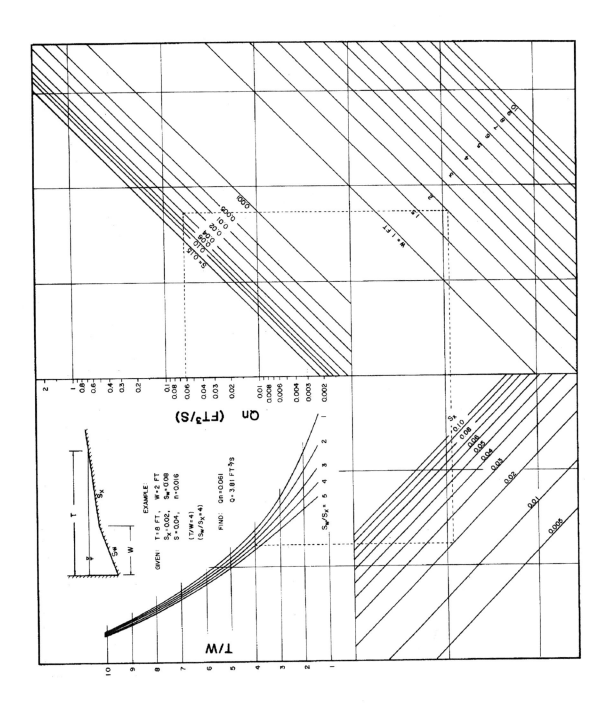

CHART 5. Flow in composite gutter sections.

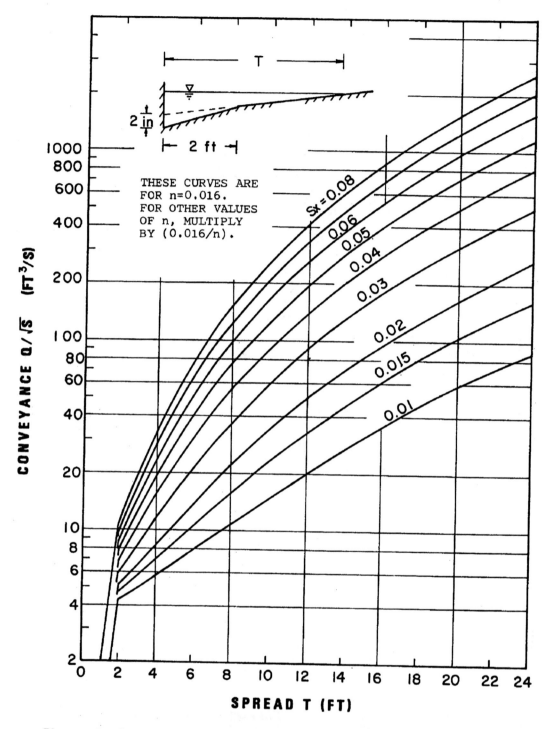

Figure 3. Conveyance–Spread curves for a composite gutter section.

28

5.4   Flow in Sag Vertical Curves

The spread of water in sag vertical curves is of concern because occasional water on the pavement is hazardous. Spread on the pavement should be examined where the slope is relatively flat at either side of the low point of a sag vertical curve to determine whether the spread is acceptable. It is suggested that spread be checked at a gradient of 0.3 percent.

Example 6:

Given: Q = 3.0 ft^3/s
        n = 0.015
        S_x = 0.025
        Qn = 0.045 ft^3/s
        S = 0.003

Find: T

Solution:
        T = 12 ft (Chart 3)

If, as in the example 4, section 5.1, the design spread is 8 ft, consideration should be given to reducing the gutter flow approaching the low point. Sag vertical curves and measures for reducing spread are further discussed in sections 6 and 8.

5.5   Shallow Swale Sections

Where curbs are not needed for traffic control, it may sometimes be advantageous to use a small swale section of circular or V-shape to convey runoff from the pavement in order to avoid the introduction of a curb. As an example, it is often necessary to control pavement runoff on fills in order to protect the embankment from erosion. Small swale sections may have sufficient capacity to convey the flow to a location suitable for interception and controlled release, as illustrated in figure 4. Chart 3 can be used to compute flow in a shallow V-section and Chart 6 is provided for part-circle sections. Examples 7 and 8 illustrate the procedures.

Example 7:

Determine whether it is feasible to use a shallow swale section in an 8-ft shoulder, given the following conditions:

Figure 4.   Use of a shallow swale in lieu of a curb.

Given: T = 8 ft
         Q = 1.5 ft^3/s
         S = 0.01
         n = 0.016

Find: Depth of V-section swale and cross slope required

Solution:

S_x = 0.021 (Chart 3)

$$S_x = \frac{S_{x1}\ S_{x2}}{S_{x1} + S_{x2}} = 0.021$$

Let $S_{x1} = S_{x2}$

Then $\dfrac{(S_{x1})^2}{2S_{x1}} = 0.021$

and

$S_{x1} = 0.042;\quad d = 4 \times 0.042 = 0.17$ ft

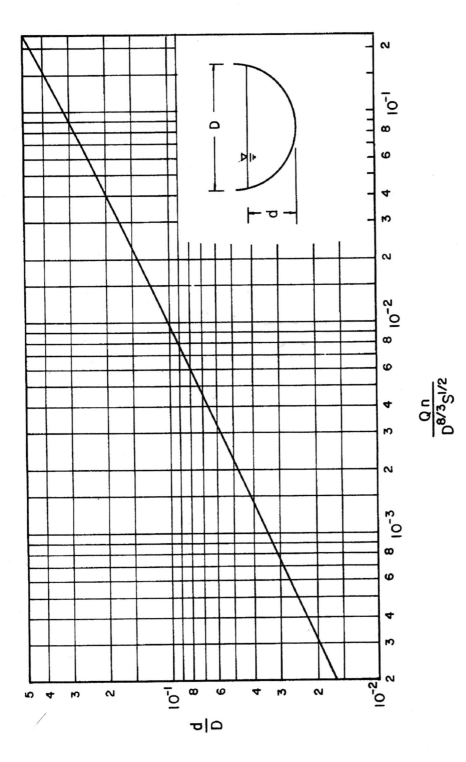

CHART 6. Conveyance in circular channels.

31

A swale section 8 ft wide and 0.17 ft deep with an average foreslope and backslope of 0.04 ft/ft will be adequate to protect the backslope.

Example 8:

Given the conditions in example 7, determine the depth and top width of a circular swale with a diameter of 5 ft.

Given: S = 0.01
        n = 0.016
        Q = 1.5 ft^3/s

Find: d, T

Solution:
        D = 5 ft

$$\frac{Qn}{D^{8/3}S^{1/2}} = \frac{1.5 \times 0.016}{73.1 \times 0.1} = 0.0032$$

        d/D = 0.06 (Chart 6)
        d = 0.30 ft

$$T = 2[2.5^2 - (2.5 - 0.30)^2]^{1/2} = 2(6.25 - 4.84)^{1/2}$$
$$= 2.4 \text{ ft}$$

A swale with a radius of 2.5 ft and a top width of 2.4 ft will convey a flow of 1.5 ft^3/s at approximately 0.3 ft of depth.

5.6 Relative Flow Capacities

The examples in sections 5.1 and 5.2 illustrate the capacity advantage of a depressed gutter section. The capacity of the section with a depressed gutter in the examples is 50 percent greater than that of the section with a straight cross slope with all other parameters held constant. A straight cross slope of 3 percent would have approximately the same capacity as the composite section with a cross slope of 2.5 percent and a gutter slope of 10.8 percent.

Equation (4), section 5.0, can be used to examine the relative effects of changing the values of spread, cross slope, and longitudinal slope on the capacity of a section with a straight cross slope.

$$Q = \frac{0.56}{n} S_x^{1.67} S^{0.5} T^{2.67} \tag{4}$$

Let $k_1 = \dfrac{n}{0.56 \; S^{0.5} \; T^{2.67}}$

Then $S_x^{1.67} = k_1 Q$

To examine the effects of cross slope on gutter capacity, the following ratio is plotted in figure 5:

$$\left(\frac{S_{x1}}{S_{x2}}\right)^{1.67} = \frac{k_1 Q_1}{k_1 Q_2} = \frac{Q_1}{Q_2}$$

The effects of changing the longitudinal slope on gutter capacity are plotted in figure 5 from the following relationship:

Let $k_2 = \dfrac{n}{0.56 \; S_x^{1.67} \; T^{2.67}}$

Then $\left(\dfrac{S_1}{S_2}\right)^{0.5} = \dfrac{Q_1}{Q_2}$

The following relationship is plotted in figure 5 to illustrate the effect of changes in the width of spread:

Let $k_3 = \dfrac{n}{0.56 \; S_x^{1.67} \; S^{0.5}}$

$$\left(\frac{T_1}{T_2}\right)^{2.67} = \frac{Q_1}{Q_2}$$

As illustrated by figure 5, the effects of spread on gutter capacity are greater than the effects of cross slope and longitudinal slope. This is to be expected because of the larger exponent. The magnitude of the effect is demonstrated by the fact that gutter capacity with a 10-ft (3.05 m) spread is 11.6 times greater than with a 4-ft (1.22 m) spread and 3.9 times greater than at a spread of 6 ft (1.83 m).

The effects of cross slope are also relatively great as illustrated by a comparison of gutter capacities with different cross slopes. At a cross slope of 4 percent, a gutter has 10 times the capacity of a gutter of 1 percent cross slope. A gutter at 4 percent cross slope has 2.2 times the capacity of a gutter at 2.5 percent cross slope. A gutter with a cross slope

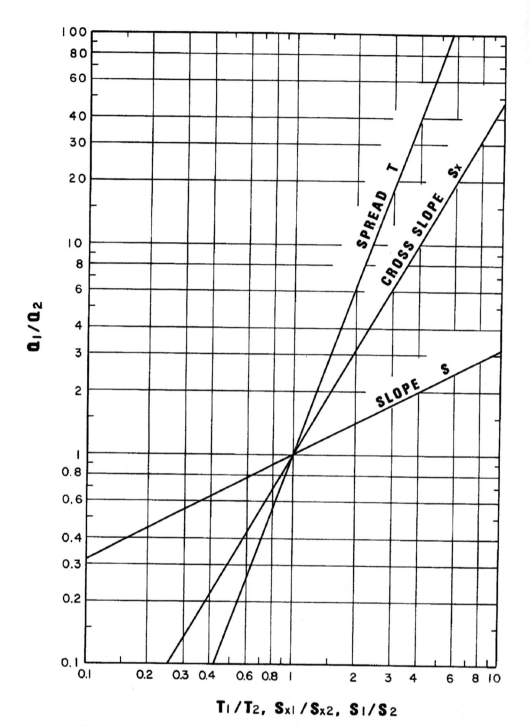

Figure 5. Relative effects of spread, cross slope, and longitudinal slope on gutter flow capacity.

of 6 percent has 6.3 times the capacity of a gutter at a cross slope of 2 percent.

Little latitude is generally available to vary longitudinal slope in order to increase gutter capacity, but slope changes which change gutter capacity are frequent. Figure 5 shows that a change from S = 0.04 to 0.02 will reduce gutter capacity to 71 percent of the capacity at S = 0.04. The capacity at extremely flat gradient sections, as on the approaches to the low point in a sag vertical curve, can also be compared with the capacity of the gutter on the approach gradients. If an approach gradient is 2 percent, the capacity of the gutter in the sag vertical curve where the gradient is 0.35 percent is 42 percent of the capacity on the approach grades.

6.0 PAVEMENT DRAINAGE INLETS

Inlets used for the drainage of highway surfaces can be divided into three major classes. These three major classes are: (1) curb-opening inlets, (2) gutter inlets, and (3) combination inlets. Each major class has many variations in design and may be installed with or without a depression of the gutter.

Curb-opening inlets are vertical openings in the curb covered by a top slab.

Gutter inlets include grate inlets consisting of an opening in the gutter covered by one or more grates, and slotted inlets consisting of a pipe cut along the longitudinal axis with a grate of spacer bars to form slot openings.

Combination inlets usually consist of both a curb-opening inlet and a grate inlet placed in a side-by-side configuration, but the curb opening may be located in part upstream of the grate.

Perspective drawings of the three classes of inlets are shown in figures 6 and 7.

Inlet interception capacity has been investigated by several agencies and manufacturers of grates. Hydraulic tests on grate inlets and slotted inlets included in this Circular were conducted by the Bureau of Reclamation for the Federal Highway Administration. Four of the grates selected for testing were rated highest in bicycle safety tests, three have designs and bar spacing similar to those proven bicycle-safe, and a parallel bar grate was used as a standard with which to compare the performance of the others.

References (3), (4), (5), and (6) are reports resulting from this grate inlet research study. Figures 8 through 13 show the inlet grates for which design procedures were developed for this Circular. For ease in identification, the following descriptive short nomenclature has been adopted:

P - 1-7/8 - Parallel bar grate with bar spacing 1-7/8-in on center (figure 8)

P - 1-7/8 - 4 - Parallel bar grate with bar spacing 1-7/8-in on center and 3/8-in diameter lateral rods spaced at 4-in on center (figure 8)

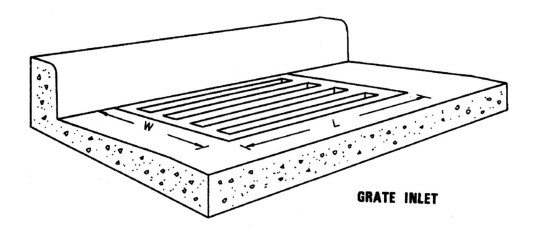

GRATE INLET

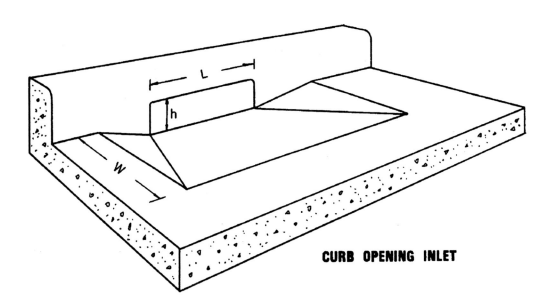

CURB OPENING INLET

Figure 6. Perspective views of grate and curb-opening inlets.

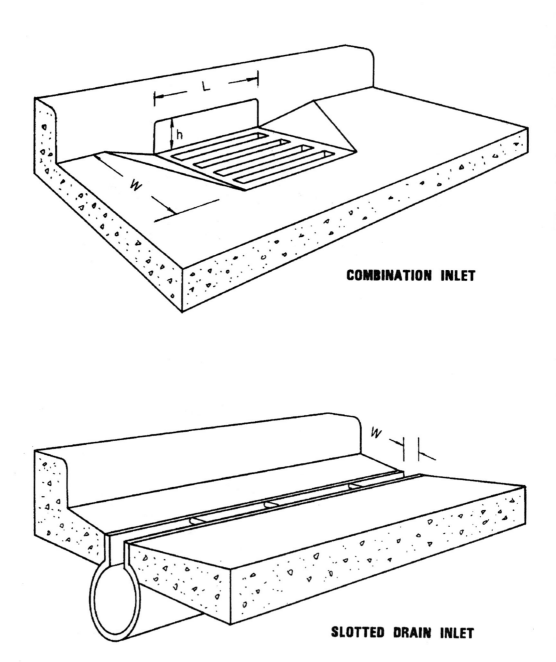

COMBINATION INLET

SLOTTED DRAIN INLET

Figure 7. Perspective views of combination inlet and slotted drain inlet.

38

P - 1-1/8 - Parallel bar grate with 1-1/8-in on center bar spacing (figure 9)

CV - 3-1/4 - 4-1/4 - Curved vane grate with 3-1/4-in longitudinal bar and 4-1/4-in transverse bar spacing on center (figure 10)

45 - 3-1/4 - 4 - 45° tilt-bar grate with 2-1/4-in longitudinal bar and 4-in transverse bar spacing on center (figure 11)

45 - 3-1/4 - 4 - 45° tilt-bar with 3-1/4-in and 4-in on center longitudinal and lateral bar spacing, respectively (figure 11)

30 - 3-1/4 - 4 - 30° tilt-bar grate with 3-1/4-in and 4-in on center longitudinal and lateral bar spacing, respectively (figure 12)

Reticuline - "honeycomb" pattern of lateral bars and longitudinal bearing bars (figure 13).

The interception capacity of curb-opening inlets has also been investigated by several agencies. Design procedures adopted for this Circular are largely derived from experimental work at Colorado State University for the Federal Highway Administration, as reported in reference (14) and from reference (15).

6.1 Factors Affecting Inlet Interception Capacity and Efficiency on Continuous Grades

Inlet interception capacity is the flow intercepted by an inlet under a given set of conditions. Under changed conditions, the interception capacity of a given inlet changes. The efficiency of an inlet is the percent of total flow that the inlet will intercept under a given set of conditions. The efficiency of an inlet changes with changes in cross slope, longitudinal slope, total gutter flow, and, to a lesser extent, pavement roughness. In mathematical form, efficiency, E, is defined by the following equation:

$$E = \frac{Q_i}{Q} \tag{5}$$

where: Q = total gutter flow, ft^3/s (m^3/s)

Q_i = intercepted flow, ft^3/s (m^3/s

Flow that is not intercepted by an inlet is termed carryover or bypass, (Q_b):

39

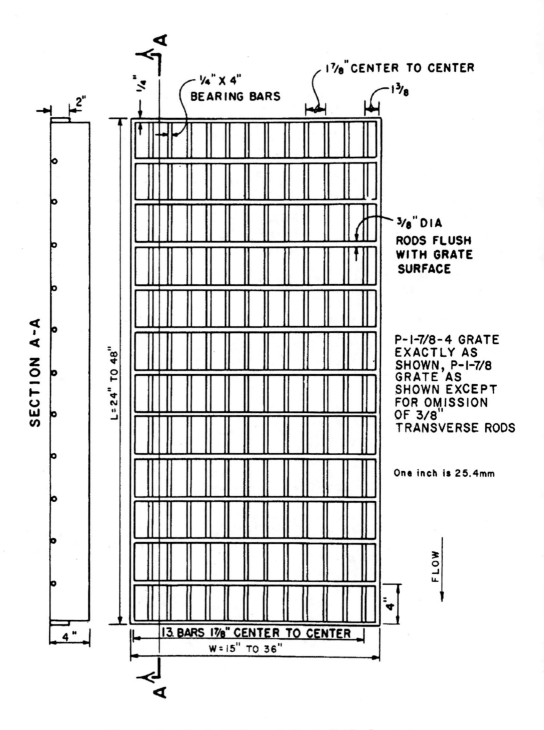

Figure 8. P-1-7/8 and P-1-7/8-4 grates.

40

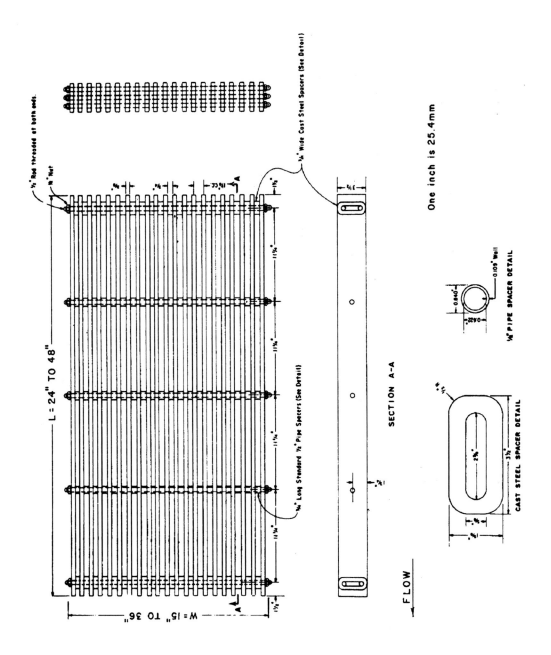

Figure 9. P-1-1/8 grate.

One inch is 25.4mm

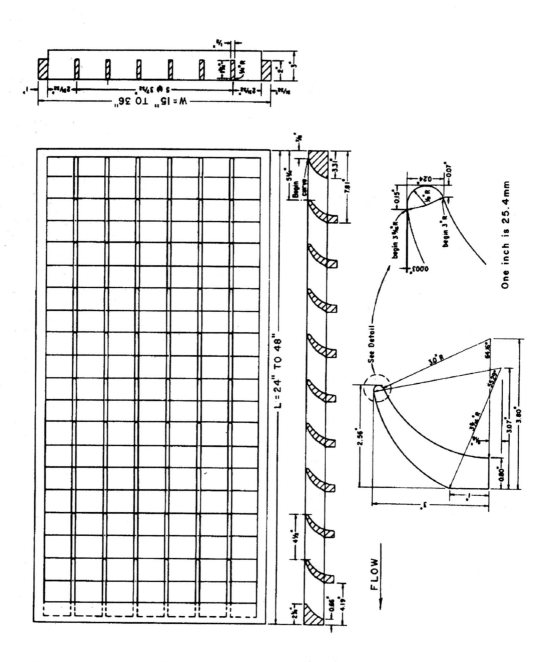

Figure 10. Curved vane grate.

42

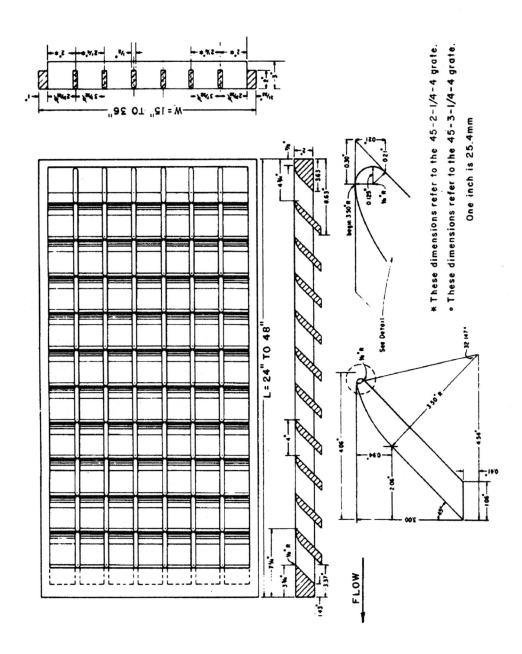

Figure 11. 45° Tilt-bar grate.

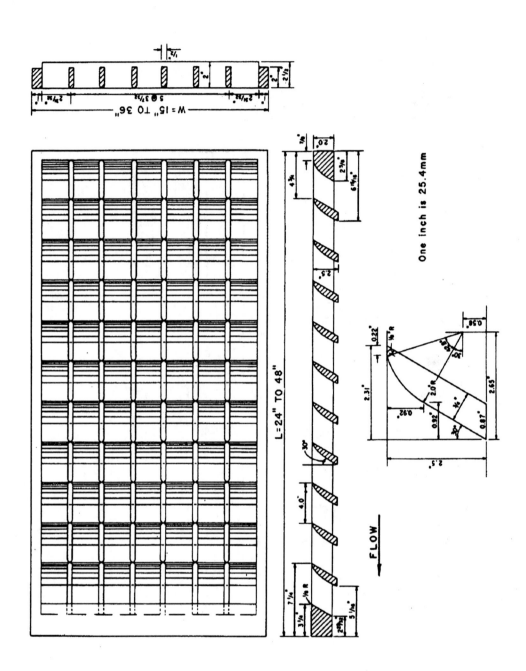

Figure 12. 30° Tilt-bar grate.

One inch is 25.4mm

44

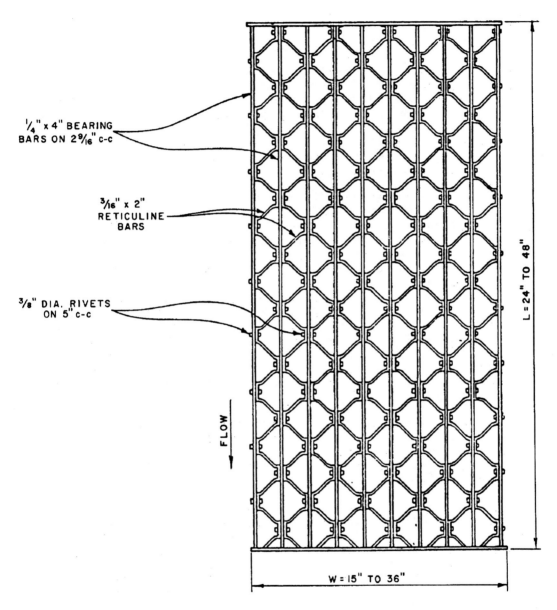

¼" x 4" BEARING
BARS ON 2⁹⁄₁₆" c-c

³⁄₁₆" x 2"
RETICULINE
BARS

³⁄₈" DIA. RIVETS
ON 5" c-c

FLOW

L = 24" TO 48"

W = 15" TO 36"

One inch is 25.4mm

Figure 13. Reticuline grate.

45

$$Q_b = Q - Q_i \qquad\qquad (6)$$

The interception capacity of all inlet configurations increases with increasing flow rates, and inlet efficiency generally decreases with increasing flow rates.

Factors affecting gutter flow also affect inlet interception capacity. The depth of water next to the curb is the major factor in the interception capacity of both gutter inlets and curb-opening inlets. The interception capacity of a grate inlet depends on the amount of water flowing over the grate, the size and configuration of the grate and the velocity of flow in the gutter. The efficiency of a grate is dependent on the same factors and total flow in the gutter.

Interception capacity of a curb-opening inlet is largely dependent on flow depth at the curb and curb opening length. Effective flow depth at the curb and consequently, curb-opening inlet interception capacity and efficiency, is increased by the use of a gutter depression at the curb-opening or a depressed gutter to increase the proportion of the total flow adjacent to the curb. Top slab supports placed flush with the curb line can substantially reduce the interception capacity of curb openings. Tests have shown that such supports reduce the effectiveness of openings downstream of the support by as much as 50 percent and, if debris is caught at the support, interception by the downstream portion of the opening may be reduced to near zero. If intermediate top slab supports are used, they should be recessed several inches from the curb line and rounded in shape as shown in figure 14.

Slotted inlets function in essentially the same manner as curb opening inlets, i.e., as weirs with flow entering from the side. Interception capacity is dependent on flow depth and inlet length. Efficiency is dependent on flow depth, inlet length and total gutter flow.

The interception capacity of a combination inlet consisting of a grate placed alongside a curb opening does not differ materially from that of a grate only. Interception capacity and efficiency are dependent on the same factors which affect grate capacity and efficiency. A combination inlet consisting of a curb-opening inlet placed upstream of a grate has a capacity equal to that of the curb-opening length upstream of the grate plus that of the grate, taking into account the reduced spread and depth of flow over the grate because of the interception by the curb opening. This inlet configuration has the added advantage of intercepting debris that might otherwise clog the grate and deflect water away from the inlet.

Figure 14.   Curb-opening inlet with intermediate
top slab supports.

A combination inlet consisting of a slotted inlet upstream
of a grate might appear to have advantages where 100 percent
interception is necessary. However, grates intercept little more
than frontal flow and would usually need to be more than 3-ft
(0.9 m) wide to contribute significantly to the interception
capacity of the combination inlet. A more practical solution
would be to use a slotted inlet of sufficient length to intercept
total flow.

6.2   Factors Affecting Inlet Interception Capacity in Sag Locations

Grate inlets in sag vertical curves operate as weirs up to
depths dependent on grate size and configuration and as orifices
at greater depths. Between weir and orifice flow depths, a
transition from weir to orifice flow occurs. The perimeter and
clear opening area of the grate and the depth of water at the
curb affect inlet capacity. The capacity at a given depth can be
severely affected if trash collects on the grate and reduces the
effective perimeter or clear opening area.

Curb-opening inlets operate as weirs in sag vertical curve locations up to a depth equal to the opening height. At depths above 1.4 times the opening height, the inlet operates as an orifice and between these depths, transition between weir and orifice flow occurs. The curb-opening height and length, and water depth at the curb affect inlet capacity. At a given flow rate, the effective water depth at the curb can be increased by the use of a continuously depressed gutter, by use of a locally depressed curb opening, or by use of an increased cross slope, thus decreasing the width of spread at the inlet.

Slotted inlets operate as orifices in sag locations where the depth at the upstream edge of the slot is greater than about 0.4 ft (0.12 m). Transition flow exists at lesser depths, and an empirical orifice equation derived from experimental data can be used to compute interception capacity. Interception capacity varies with flow depth, slope, width, and length at a given spread.

6.3 Comparison of Interception Capacity of Inlets on Grade

In order to compare the interception capacity and efficiency of various inlets on grade, it is necessary to fix two variables that affect capacity and efficiency and investigate the effects of varying the other factor. Figure 15 shows a comparison of curb-opening inlets, grates, and slotted drain inlets with gutter

flow fixed at 3 ft^3/s (0.08 m^3/s), cross slope fixed at 3 percent, and longitudinal slope varied up to 10 percent. Conclusions drawn from an analysis of this figure are not necessarily transferable to other flow rates or cross slopes, but some inferences can be drawn that are applicable to other sets of conditions. Grate configurations used for interception capacity comparisons in this figure are described in section 6.

Figure 15 illustrates the effects of flow depth at the curb and curb-opening length on curb-opening inlet interception capacity and efficiency. All of the curb-opening inlets shown in the figure lose interception capacity and efficiency as the longitudinal slope is increased because spread on the pavement and depth at the curb become smaller as velocity increases. It is accurate to conclude that curb-opening inlet interception capacity and efficiency would increase with steeper cross slopes. It is also accurate to conclude that interception capacity would increase and inlet efficiency decreases with increased flow rates.

The effect of depth at the curb is also illustrated by a comparison of the interception capacity and efficiency of depressed and undepressed curb-opening inlets. A 5-ft depressed

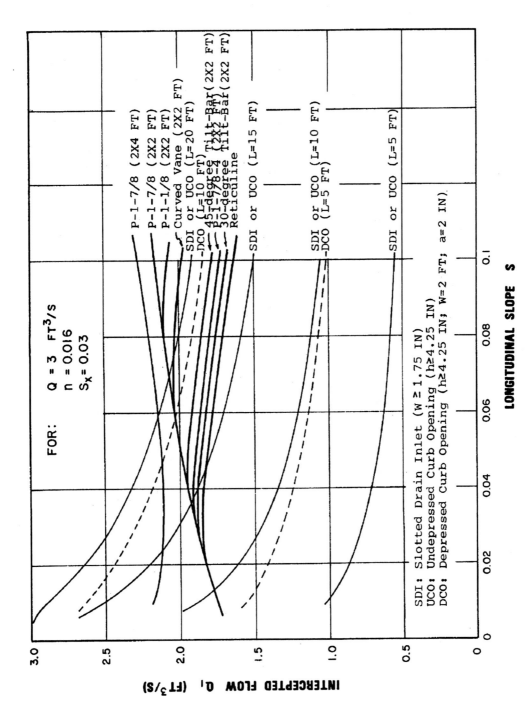

Figure 15. Comparison of inlet interception capacity, slope variable.

FOR:
Q = 3 FT³/s
n = 0.016
Sₓ = 0.03

P-1-7/8 (2X4 FT)
P-1-7/8 (2X2 FT)
P-1-1/8 (2X2 FT)
Curved Vane (2X2 FT)
SDI or UCO (L=20 FT)
DCO (L=10 FT)
45-degree Tilt-Bar (2X2 FT)
P-1-7/8-4 (2X2 FT)
30-degree Tilt-Bar (2X2 FT)
Reticuline

SDI or UCO (L=15 FT)

SDI or UCO (L=10 FT)
DCO (L=5 FT)

SDI or UCO (L=5 FT)

LONGITUDINAL SLOPE S

INTERCEPTED FLOW Qᵢ (FT³/S)

SDI: Slotted Drain Inlet (w ≥ 1.75 IN)
UCO: Undepressed Curb Opening (h≥4.25 IN)
DCO: Depressed Curb Opening (h≥4.25 IN; W=2 FT; a=2 IN).

49

curb-opening inlet has about 67 percent more interception capacity than an undepressed inlet at 2 percent slope, 3 percent cross slope, and 3 ft^3/s (0.08 m^3/s) and about 79 percent more interception capacity at an 8 percent slope.

At low velocities, all of the water flowing in the section of gutter occupied by the grate, called frontal flow, is intercepted by grate inlets, and a small portion of the flow along the length of the grate, termed side flow, is intercepted. Water begins to skip or splash over the grate at velocities dependent on the grate configuration. Figure 15 shows that interception capacity and efficiency is reduced at slopes steeper than the slope at which splash-over begins. Splash-over for the less efficient grates begins at the slope at which the interception capacity curve begins to deviate from the curve of the more efficient grates. All of the 2-ft by 2-ft (0.61 m x 0.61 m) grates have equal interception capacity and efficiency at a flow rate of 3 ft^3/s (0.08 m^3/s), cross slope of 3 percent, and slope of 2 percent. At slopes steeper than 2 percent, splash-over occurs on the reticuline grate and the interception capacity is reduced. At a slope of 6 percent, velocities are such that splash-over occurs on all except the curved vane and parallel bar grates. From these performance characteristics curves, it can be concluded that parallel-bar grates and the curved vane grate are relatively efficient at higher velocities and the reticuline grate is least efficient. At low velocities, the grates perform equally.

The capacity and efficiency of grates increase with increased slope and velocity, if splash-over does not occur, in contrast with slotted inlets and curb-opening inlets. This is because frontal flow increases with increased velocity and all frontal flow will be intercepted if splash-over does not occur.

Interception capacity and efficiency of curb-opening and slotted inlets decrease with increased slope because of reduced flow depths at the curb. Long curb-opening and slotted inlets compare favorable with grates in interception capacity and efficiency for conditions illustrated in figure 15.

Figure 15 also illustrates that interception by longer grates would not be substantially greater than interception by 2-ft by 2-ft (0.61 x 0.61 m) grates. In order to capture more of the flow, wider grates would be needed.

Figure 16 can be used for further study and comparisons of inlet interception capacity and efficiency. It shows, for example, that at a 6 percent slope, splash-over begins at about 0.7 ft^3/s (0.02 m^3/s) on a reticuline grate. It also illustrates

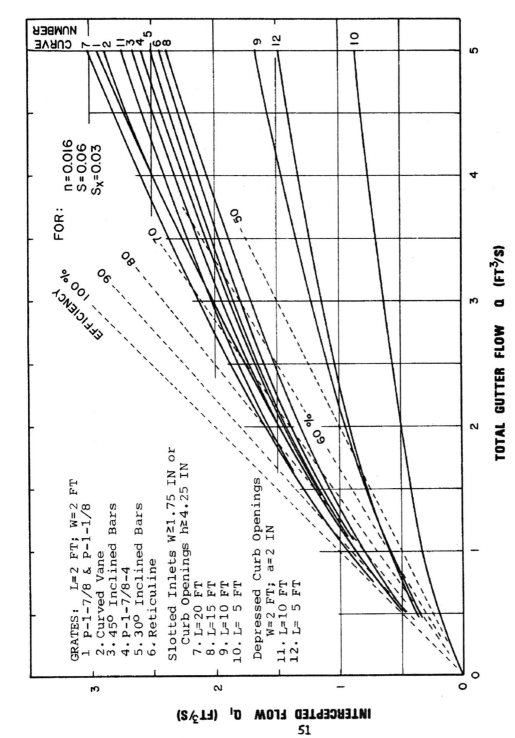

Figure 16. Comparison of inlet interception capacity, flow rate variable.

51

that the interception capacity of all inlets increases and inlet efficiency decreases with increased discharge. Figure 15, with a fixed flow rate, shows decreasing interception capacity and efficiency for curb openings and slotted inlets, and increasing capacity and efficiency for grates with increased slopes until splash-over begins.

This comparison of inlet interception capacity and efficiency neglects the effects of debris and clogging on the various inlets. All types of inlets, including curb-opening inlets, are subject to clogging, some being much more susceptible than others. Attempts to simulate clogging tendencies in the laboratory have not been notably successful, except to demonstrate the importance of parallel bar spacing in debris handling efficiency. Grates with wider spacings of longitudinal bars pass debris more efficiently. Except for reticuline grates, grates with lateral bar spacing of less than 4-in (0.10 m) were not tested so conclusions cannot be drawn from tests concerning debris handling capabilities of many grates currently in use. Problems with clogging are largely local since the amount of debris varies significantly from one locality to another. Some localities must contend with only a small amount of debris while others experience extensive clogging of drainage inlets. Since partial clogging of inlets on grade rarely causes major problems, allowances should not be made for reduction in inlet interception capacity except where local experience indicates an allowance is advisable.

7.0 INTERCEPTION CAPACITY OF INLETS ON GRADE

The interception capacity of inlets on grade is dependent on factors discussed in section 6.1. In this section, new design charts for inlets on grade and procedures for using the charts are presented for the various inlet configurations.

Charts for grate inlet interception have been made general and are applicable to all grate inlets tested for the Federal Highway Administration (3 through 6). The chart for frontal flow interception is based on test results which show that grates intercept all of the frontal flow until a velocity is reached at which water begins to splash over the grate. At velocities greater than "splash-over" velocity, grate efficiency in intercepting frontal flow is diminished. Grates also intercept a portion of the flow along the length of the grate, or the side flow. A chart is provided to determine side-flow interception.

One set of charts is provided for slotted inlets and curb-opening inlets, because these inlets are both side-flow weirs. The equation developed for determining the length of inlet required for total interception fits the test data for both types of inlets.

A procedure for determining the interception capacity of combination inlets is also presented for cases where it would differ materially from the interception capacity of a grate only and for use where partial or total clogging of the grate is assumed.

7.1 Grate Inlets

Grates are effective highway pavement drainage inlets where clogging with debris is not a problem. Where debris is a problem, consideration should be given to debris handling efficiency rankings from laboratory tests in which an attempt was made to qualitatively simulate field conditions (3). Debris handling efficiencies were based on the total number of simulated "leaves" arriving at the grate and the number passed. Results of the tests are summarized in table 4.

Grate inlets will intercept all of the gutter flow passing over the grate, or the frontal flow, if the grate is sufficiently long and the gutter flow velocity is low. Only a portion of the frontal flow will·be intercepted if the velocity is high or the grate is short and splash-over occurs. A part of the flow along the side of the grate will be intercepted, dependent on the cross

Table 4. Average debris handling efficiencies of
         grates tested.

Rank	Grate	Longitudinal slope	
		0.005	0.04
1	CV - 3-1/4 - 4-1/4	46	61
2	30 - 3-1/4 - 4	44	55
3	45 - 3-1/4 - 4	43	48
4	P - 1-7/8	32	32
5	P - 1-7/8 - 4	18	28
6	45 - 2-1/4 - 4	16	23
7	Recticuline	12	16
8	P - 1-1/8	9	20

slope of the pavement, the length of the grate, and flow
velocity.

The ratio of frontal flow to total gutter flow, E_o, for a
straight cross slope is expressed by equation (7):

$$E_o = \frac{Q_w}{Q} = 1 - (1 - W/T)^{2.67} \tag{7}$$

where: Q = total gutter flow
        Q_w = flow in width W, ft^3/s (m^3/s)
        W = width of depressed gutter or grate, ft (m)
        T = total spread of water in the gutter, ft (m)

Chart 4, section 5.2, provides a graphical solution of E_o
for either straight cross slopes or depressed gutter sections.

The ratio of side flow, Q_s, to total gutter flow is:

$$\frac{Q_s}{Q} = 1 - \frac{Q_w}{Q} = 1 - E_o \tag{8}$$

The ratio of frontal flow intercepted to total frontal flow,
R_f, is expressed by equation (9):

$$R_f = 1 - 0.09 (V - V_o) \tag{9}$$

where: V = velocity of flow in the gutter, ft/s (m/s)
        V_o = gutter velocity where splash-over first occurs

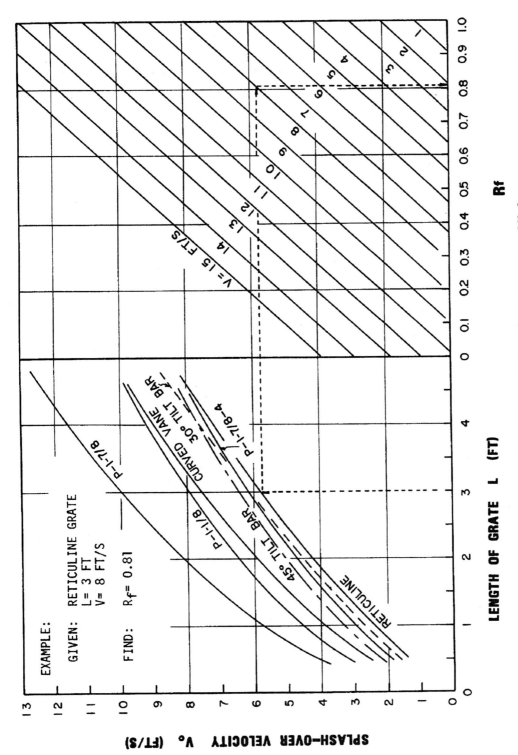

CHART 7. Grate inlet frontal flow interception efficiency.

This ratio is equivalent to frontal flow interception efficiency. Chart 7 provides a solution of equation (9) which takes into account grate length, bar configuration and gutter velocity at which splash-over occurs. The gutter velocity needed to use Chart 7 is total gutter flow divided by the area of flow.

The ratio of side flow intercepted to total side flow, R_s, or side flow interception efficiency, is expressed by equation (10):

$$R_s = 1/(1 + \frac{0.15V^{1.8}}{S_x L^{2.3}})$$ (10)

where: L = length of the grate, ft (m)

Chart 8 provides a solution of equation (10).

A deficiency in developing empirical equations and charts from experimental data is evident in Chart 8. The fact that a grate will intercept all or almost all of the side flow where the velocity is low and the spread only slightly exceeds the grate width is not reflected in the Chart. Error due to this deficiency is very small. In fact, where velocities are high, side flow interception can be neglected entirely without significant error.

The efficiency, E, of a grate is expressed as equation (11):

$$E = R_f E_o + R_s(1 - E_o)$$ (11)

The first term on the right side of equation (11) is the ratio of intercepted frontal flow to total gutter flow, and the second term is the ratio of intercepted side flow to total side flow. The second term is insignificant with high velocities and short grates.

The interception capacity of a grate inlet on grade is equal to the efficiency of the grate multiplied by the total gutter flow:

$$Q_i = EQ = Q[R_f E_o + R_s(1 - E_o)]$$ (12)

Use of Charts 7 and 8 is illustrated in the following examples.

Example 9:

Given: Data from example 5 in section 5.2

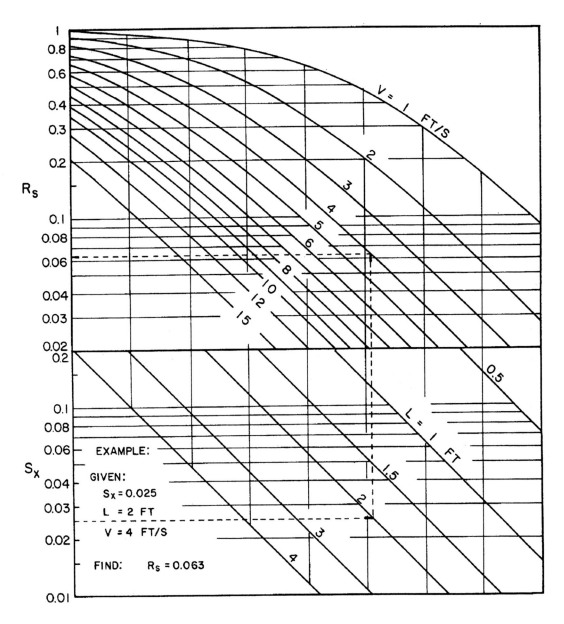

CHART 8. Grate inlet side flow interception efficiency.

Find: Interception capacity of:
        (1) a curved vane grate, and
        (2) a reticuline grate 2-ft long and 2-ft wide

Solution:
        From example 5, section 5.2:
        W = 2 ft
        Gutter depression = 2 in
        T = 8 ft
        S = 0.01
        S_x = 0.025
        E_o = 0.69
        Q = 3.0 ft^3/s
        V = 3.1 ft/s

        (1)   Curved Vane Grate: R_f = 1.0 (Chart 7)
        (2)   Reticuline Grate: R_f = 1.0 Chart 7)

        Both grates: R_s = 0.1 (Chart 8)

        From Equation 12:
        Q_i = 3.0[1.0 x 0.69 + 0.1(1 - 0.69)] = 3(.69 + 0.03)

            = 2.2 ft^3/s

        The interception capacity of a curved vane grate is the same
as that for a reticuline grate for the stated conditions. Note
that if side interception were neglected, the results would be
within the range of accuracy of the runoff estimation method and
gutter flow computations.

Example 10:
Given: T = 10 ft
        S_x = 0.025
        S = 0.04
        n = 0.016
        Bicycle traffic is not permitted

Find: Interception capacity:
        (1)   P - 1-7/8 grate; width = 2 ft; length = 2 ft
        (2)   Reticuline grate; width = 2 ft; length = 2 ft
        (3)   Use length, L = 4 ft

Solution:
        Q = 6.6 ft^3/s (Chart 3)
        W/T = 2/10 = 0.20
        E_o = 0.46 (Chart 4)
        V = 5.3 ft/s (Chart 2)

(1) $R_f = 1.0$ (P – 1-7/8 grate) (Chart 7)
(2) $R_f = 0.9$ (Reticuline grate) (Chart 7)
(3) $R_f = 1.0$ (Both grates)

(1) and (2) $R_s = 0.04$ (Chart 8)
(3) $R_s = 0.17$ (Both grates)

From equation (12):
(1) $Q_i = 6.6[1.0 \times 0.46 + 0.04(1 - 0.46)]$
$= 6.6(0.46 + .02) = 3.2 \text{ ft}^3/\text{s}$ (P – 1-7/8)
(2) $Q_i = 6.6[0.9 \times 0.46 + 0.04(1 - 0.46)]$

$= 6.6(0.41 + 0.02) = 2.8 \text{ ft}^3/\text{s}$ (reticuline)
(3) $Q_i = 6.6[0.46 + 0.17(0.54)]$

$= 3.6 \text{ ft}^3/\text{s}$ (both grates)

The parallel bar grate will intercept about 14 percent more flow than the reticuline grate or 48 percent of the total flow as opposed to 42 percent for the reticuline grate. Increasing the length of the grates would not be cost-effective because the increase in side flow interception is small.

It may be desirable for agencies to develop design curves for the standard grates used. A step-by-step procedure is provided in Appendix E for this purpose.

7.2 Curb-Opening Inlets

Curb-opening inlets are effective in the drainage of highway pavements where flow depth at the curb is sufficient for the inlet to perform efficiently, as discussed in section 6.1. Curb openings are relatively free of clogging tendencies and offer little interference to traffic operation. They are a viable alternative to grates in many locations where grates would be in traffic lanes or would be hazardous for pedestrians or bicyclists.

The length of curb-opening inlet required for total interception of gutter flow on a pavement section with a straight cross slope is expressed by equation (13):

$$L_T = KQ^{0.42}S^{0.3}\left(\frac{1}{nS_x}\right)^{0.6} \qquad (13)$$

where: $K = 0.6$ (0.076 in SI)
L_T = curb opening length required to intercept 100 percent of the gutter flow

The efficiency of curb-opening inlets shorter than the length required for total interception is expressed by equation (14):

$$E = 1 - (1 - L/L_T)^{1.8} \qquad (14)$$

where: L = curb-opening length, ft (m)

Chart 9 is a nomograph for the solution of equation (13), and Chart 10 provides a solution of equation (14).

The length of inlet required for total interception by depressed curb-opening inlets or curb-openings in depressed gutter sections can be found by the use of an equivalent cross slope, S_e, in equation (13).

$$S_e = S_x + S_w' E_o \qquad (15)$$

where: S_w' = cross slope of the gutter measured from the cross slope of the pavement, S_x

$$= (a/12W)$$

where: a = gutter depression, in (m)
E_o = ratio of flow in the depressed section to total gutter flow

E_o is the same ratio as that used to compute the frontal flow interception of a grate inlet.

It is apparent from examination of Chart 9 that the length of curb opening required for total interception can be significantly reduced by increasing the cross slope or the equivalent cross slope. The equivalent cross slope can be increased by use of a continuously depressed gutter section or a locally depressed gutter section, as in figure 17.

Using the equivalent cross slope, S_e, equation (13) becomes:

$$L_T = KQ^{0.42} S^{0.3} \left(\frac{1}{nS_e}\right)^{0.6} \qquad (16)$$

The values of K in equation (16) are the same as in equation (13).

Equation (14) is applicable with either straight cross slopes or compound cross slopes. Charts 9 and 10 are applicable to depressed curb-opening inlets using S_e rather than S_x.

Equation (15) uses the ratio, E_o, in the computation of the

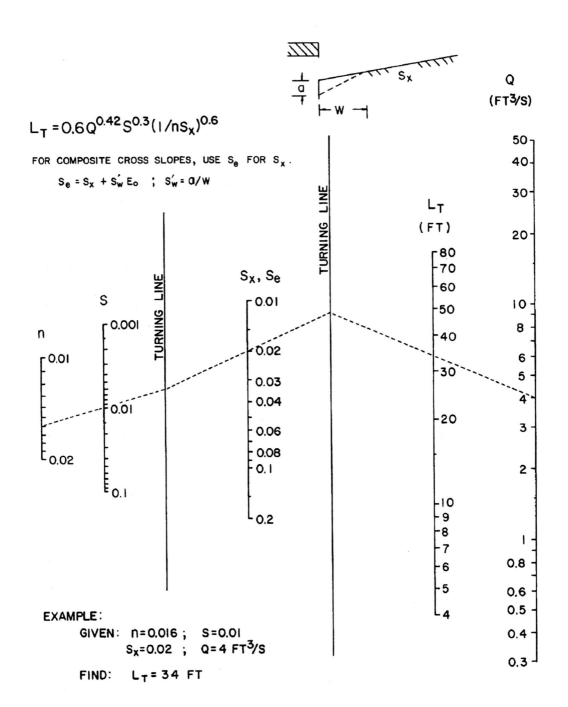

$$L_T = 0.6 Q^{0.42} S^{0.3} (1/nS_x)^{0.6}$$

FOR COMPOSITE CROSS SLOPES, USE S_e FOR S_x.

$$S_e = S_x + S_w' E_o \quad ; \quad S_w' = a/W$$

EXAMPLE:

GIVEN: n=0.016 ; S=0.01
S_x=0.02 ; Q=4 FT³/S

FIND: L_T = 34 FT

CHART 9. Curb-opening and slotted drain inlet length for total interception.

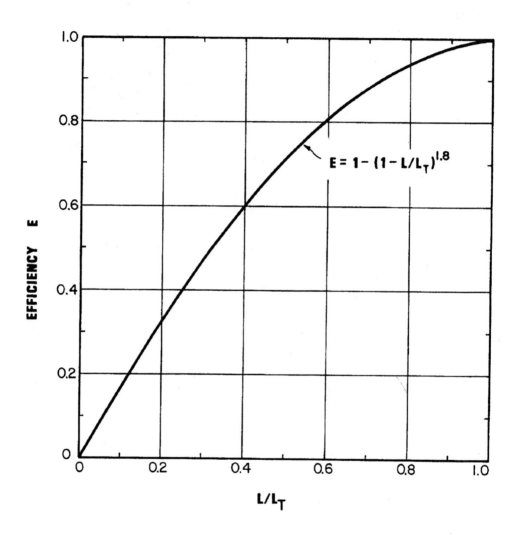

$$E = 1 - (1 - L/L_T)^{1.8}$$

CHART 10. Curb–opening and slotted drain inlet interception efficiency.

equivalent cross slope, S_e. Chart 5 can be used to determine
spread and Chart 4 can then be used to determine E_o, as
illustrated in example 11.

Figure 17.   Depressed curb-opening inlet.

Example 11:

Given: $S_x = 0.03$
          $S = 0.035$

          $Q = 5$ ft^3/s
          $n = 0.016$

Find: (1) Q_i for a 10-ft curb-opening inlet
          (2) Q_i for a depressed 10-ft curb-opening inlet
               $a = 2$ in
               $W = 2$ ft

Solution:
          (1) $T = 8$ ft (Chart 3)
               $L_T = 41$ ft (Chart 9)
               $L/L_T = 10/41 = 0.24$
               $E = 0.39$ (Chart 10)
               $Q_i = EQ = 0.39 \times 5 = 2.0$ ft^3/s

(2) $Qn = 5.0 \times 0.016 = 0.08 \text{ ft}^3/\text{s}$

$S_w/S_x = (0.03 + 0.083)/0.03 = 3.77$

$T/W = 3.5$ (Chart 5)

$T = 3.5W = 7.0 \text{ ft}$

$W/T = 2/7 = 0.29$

$E_o = 0.72$ (Chart 4)

$S_e = S_x + S_w'E_o = 0.03 + 0.083(0.72) = 0.09$

$L_T = 23 \text{ ft}$ (Chart 9)

$L/L_T = 10/23 = 0.43$

$E = 0.64$ (Chart 10)

$Q_i = 0.64 \times 5 = 3.2 \text{ ft}^3/\text{s}$

The depressed curb-opening inlet will intercept 1.6 times the flow intercepted by the undepressed curb opening and over 60 percent of the total flow.

7.3 Slotted Inlets

Wide experience with the debris handling capabilities of slotted inlets is not available. Deposition in the pipe is the problem most commonly encountered, and the inlet is accessible for cleaning with a high pressure water jet.

Slotted inlets are effective pavement drainage inlets which have a variety of applications. They can be used on curbed or uncurbed sections and offer little interference to traffic operations. An installation is illustrated in figure 18.

Flow interception by slotted inlets and curb-opening inlets is similar in that each is a side weir and the flow is subjected to lateral acceleration due to the cross slope of the pavement. Analysis of data from the Federal Highway Administration tests of slotted inlets with slot widths $\geq$ 1.75-in indicates that the length of slotted inlet required for total interception can be computed by equation (13). Chart 9 is therefore applicable for both curb-opening inlets and slotted inlets. Similarly, equation (14) is also applicable to slotted inlets and Chart 10 can be used to obtain the inlet efficiency for the selected length of inlet.

Use of Charts 9 and 10 for slotted inlets is identical to their use for curb-opening inlets. Additional examples to demonstrate the use of the charts are not provided here for that reason. It should be noted, however, that it is much less expensive to add length to a slotted inlet to increase interception capacity than it is to add length to a curb-opening inlet.

Figure 18. Slotted drain inlet at an intersection.

7.4 Combination Inlets

The interception capacity of a combination inlet consisting of a curb opening and grate placed side-by-side, as shown in figure 19, is not appreciable greater than that of the grate alone. Capacity is computed by neglecting the curb opening. A combination inlet is sometimes used with the curb opening or a part of the curb opening placed upstream of the grate as illustrated in figure 20. The curb opening in such an installation intercepts debris which might otherwise clog the grate and has been termed a "sweeper" by some. A combination inlet with a curb opening upstream of the grate has an interception capacity equal to the sum of the two inlets, except that the frontal flow and thus the interception capacity of the grate is reduced by interception by the curb opening.

Figure 19. Combination curb-opening, 45° tilt-bar
grate inlet.

The following examples illustrate computation of the interception capacity of a combination curb opening - grate inlet with
a portion of the curb opening upstream of the grate.

Example 12:

Given: $Q = 7$ ft^3/s
        $S = 0.04$
        $S_x = 0.03$
        $n = 0.016$

Find: Interception capacity of a combination curb opening -
        grate inlet. The curb opening is 10-ft long and the
        grate is a 2-ft by 2-ft reticuline grate placed along-
        side the downstream 2-ft of the curb opening.

Solution:
        $L_T = 52$ ft (Chart 9)
        8 ft of the curb opening is upstream of the grate.

Figure 20. Combination inlet with portion of curb
opening upstream of grates.

$L/L_T = 8/52 = 0.15$
$E = 0.25$ (Chart 10)
$Q_i = 0.25 \times 7 = 1.8$ ft^3/s (interception capacity of
the curb opening upstream of the grate)

$Q - Q_i = 7 - 1.8 = 5.2$ ft^3/s (Q at the grate)

$T = 8$ (Chart 3)
$W/T = 2/8 = .25$
$E_o = 0.54$ (Chart 4)
$R_f = 0.91$ (Chart 7)
$R_s = 0.06$ (Chart 8)
$E = R_f E_o + R_s(1 - E_o) = 0.91(0.54) + 0.06(0.46) = 0.52$

$Q_i = 0.52 \times 5.2 = 2.7$ ft^3/s (interception capacity of
the grate)

Total $Q_i = 1.8 + 2.7 = 4.5$ ft^3/s

Example 13:

Given: Data from example 12.

Find: (1) Q_i for a 10-ft curb opening
         (2) Q_i for a 2 x 2 ft reticuline grate

Solution:
         (1) L_T = 52 ft (example 12)
              L/L_T = 10/52 = 0.19
              E = 0.31 (Chart 10)
              Q_i = EQ = 0.31 x 7 = 2.2 ft³/s

         (2) T = 9 ft (Chart 3)
              W/T = 2/9 = 0.22
              V = 5.7 ft/s (Chart 2)
              E_o = 0.48 (Chart 4)
              R_f = 0.89 (Chart 7)
              R_s = 0.04 (Chart 8)
              E = 0.89(0.48) + 0.04(0.52) = 0.45

              Q_i = EQ = 0.45 x 7 = 3.2 ft³/s

     The combination inlet of example 12 has twice as much
capacity as the curb opening only and 41 percent more capacity
than the grate only. The combination inlet, curb-opening inlet,
and grate inlet intercept 64 percent, 31 percent, and 46 percent
of the total gutter flow, respectively.

8.0 INTERCEPTION CAPACITY OF INLETS IN SAG LOCATIONS

Inlets in sag locations operate as weirs under low head conditions and as orifices at greater depths. Orifice flow begins at depths dependent on the grate size, the curb opening height, or the slot width of the inlet, as the case may be. At depths between those at which weir flow definitely prevails and those at which orifice flow prevails, flow is in a transition stage. At these depths, control is ill-defined and flow may fluctuate between weir and orifice control. Design procedures adopted for this Circular are based on a conservative approach to estimating the capacity of inlets in sump locations.

The efficiency of inlets in passing debris is critical in sag locations because all runoff which enters the sag must be passed through the inlet. Total or partial clogging of inlets in these locations can result in hazardous ponded conditions. Grate inlets alone are not recommended for use in sag locations because of the tendencies of grates to become clogged. Combination inlets or curb-opening inlets are recommended for use in these locations.

8.1 Grate Inlets

A grate inlet in a sag location operates as a weir to depths dependent on the bar configuration and size of the grate and as an orifice at greater depths. Grates of larger dimension and grates with more open area, i.e., with less space occupied by lateral and longitudinal bars, will operate as weirs to greater depths than smaller grates or grates with less open area.

The capacity of grate inlets operating as weirs is:

$$Q_i = C_w P d^{1.5} \qquad (17)$$

where: P = perimeter of the grate in ft (m) disregarding bars and the side against the curb
C_w = 3.0 (1.66 for SI)

The capacity of a grate inlet operating as an orifice is:

$$Q_i = C_o A (2gd)^{0.5} \qquad (18)$$

where: C_o = orifice coefficient
= 0.67
A = clear opening area of the grate, ft^2 (m^2)
g = 32.16 ft/s^2 (9.80 m/s^2)

Use of equation (18) requires the clear area of opening of the grate. Tests of three grates for the Federal Highway Administration (5) showed that for flat bar grates, such as the P - 1-7/8 - 4 and P - 1-1/8 grates, the clear opening is equal to the total area of the grate less the area occupied by longitudinal and lateral bars. The curved vane grate performed about 10 percent better than a grate with a net opening equal to the total area less the area of the bars projected on a horizontal plane. That is, the projected area of the bars in a curved vane grate is 68 percent of the total area of the grate leaving a net opening of 32 percent. The grate performed as a grate with a net opening of 35 percent. Tilt-bar grates were not tested, but extrapolation of the above results would indicate a net opening area of 34 percent for the 30-degree tilt-bar and zero for the 45-degree tilt-bar grate. Obviously, the 45-degree tilt-bar grate would have greater than zero capacity. Tilt-bar and curved vane grates are not recommended for sump locations where there is a chance that operation would be as an orifice.

Opening ratios for the grates tested and the 30-degree tilt-bar grate are given on Chart 11.

Chart 11 is a plot of equations (17) and (18) for various grate sizes. The effects of grate size on the depth at which a grate operates as an orifice is apparent from the chart. Transition from weir to orifice flow results in interception capacity less than that computed by either the weir or the orifice equation. This capacity can be approximated by drawing in a curve between the lines representing the perimeter and net area of the grate to be used.

Example 14 illustrates use of Chart 11:

Example 14:

Given: A symmetrical sag vertical curve with equal bypass from inlets upgrade of the low point; allow for 50% clogging of the grate.

Q_b = 3.6 ft^3/s

Q = 8 ft^3/s, design storm

Q_b = 4.4 ft^3/s

Q = 11 ft^3/s, check storm
T = 10 ft, design
S_x = 0.05
d = TS_x = 0.5 ft

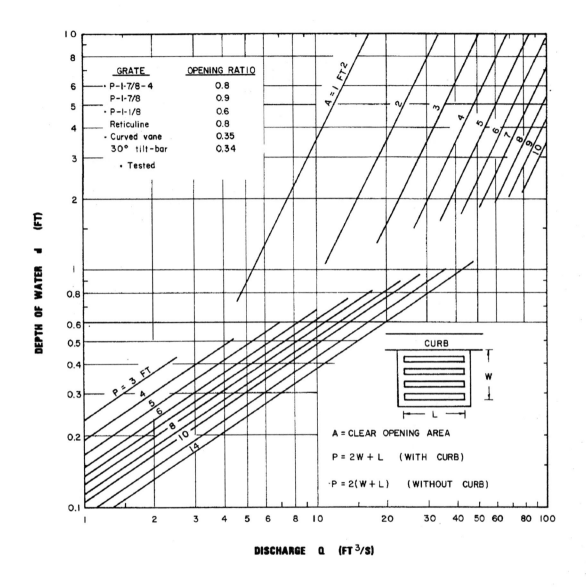

CHART 11. Grate inlet capacity in sump conditions.

Find: Grate size for design Q and depth at curb for check Q.
         Check spread at S = 0.003 on approaches to the low point.

Solution:
         From Chart 11, a grate must have a perimeter of 8 ft to

         intercept 8 ft^3/s at a depth of 0.5 ft. Some assumptions
         must be made regarding the nature of the clogging in
         order to compute the capacity of a partially clogged
         grate. If the area of a grate is 50 percent covered by
         debris so that the debris-covered portion does not con-
         tribute to interception, the effective perimeter will be
         reduced by a lesser amount than 50 percent. For example,
         if a 2-ft x 4-ft grate is clogged so that the effective
         width is 1-ft, then the perimeter, P = 1 + 4 + 1 = 6 ft,
         rather than 8 ft, the total perimeter, or 4 ft, half of
         the total perimeter. The area of the opening would be
         reduced by 50 percent and the perimeter by 25 percent.
         Therefore, assuming 50 percent clogging along the length
         of the grate, a 4 x 4, a 2 x 6, or a 3 x 5 grate would
         meet requirements of an 8-ft perimeter 50 percent clog-
         ged.

         Assuming that the installation chosen to meet design
         conditions is a double 2 x 3 ft grate, for 50 percent
         clogged conditions:

         P = 1 + 6 + 1 = 8 ft

         For design flow:
         d = 0.5 ft (Chart 11)

         For check flow:
         d = 0.6 ft (Chart 11)
         T = 12.0 ft

     At the check flow rate, ponding will extend 2 ft into a
traffic lane if the grate is 50 percent clogged in the manner
assumed.

     AASHTO geometric policy recommends a gradient of 0.3 percent
within 50 ft of the level point in a sag vertical curve.

         Check T at S = 0.003 for the design flow, and check flow:

         Q = 3.6 ft^3/s, T = 8.2 ft (design storm) (Chart 3)

         Q = 4.4 ft^3/s, T = 9 ft (check storm) (Chart 3)

72

Conclusion:

A double 2 x 3-ft grate 50 percent clogged is adequate to intercept the design flow at a spread which does not exceed design spread and spread on the approaches to the low point will not exceed design spread. However, the tendency of grate inlets to clog completely warrants consideration of a combination inlet or curb-opening inlet in a sag where ponding can occur and flanking inlets on the low gradient approaches.

8.2 Curb-Opening Inlets

The capacity of a curb-opening inlet in a sag depends on water depth at the curb, the curb opening length, and the height of the curb opening. The inlet operates as a weir to depths equal to the curb opening height and as an orifice at depths greater than 1.4 times the opening height. At depths between 1.0 and 1.4 times the opening height, flow is in a transition stage.

Spread on the pavement is the usual criterion for judging the adequacy of pavement drainage inlet design. It is also convenient and practical in the laboratory to measure depth at the curb upstream of the inlet at the point of maximum spread on the pavement. Therefore, depth at the curb measurements from experiments coincide with the depth at curb of interest to designers. The weir coefficient for a curb-opening inlet is less than the usual weir coefficient for several reasons, the most obvious of which is that depth measurements from experimental tests were not taken at the weir, and drawdown occurs between the point where measurements were made and the weir.

The weir location for a depressed curb-opening inlet is at the edge of the gutter, and the effective weir length is dependent on the width of the depressed gutter and the length of the curb opening. The weir location for a curb-opening inlet that is not depressed is at the lip of the curb opening, and its length is equal to that of the inlet. Limited experiments and extrapolation of the results of tests on depressed inlets indicate that the weir coefficient for curb-opening inlets without depression is approximately equal to that for a depressed curb-opening inlet.

The equation for the interception capacity of a depressed curb-opening inlet operating as a weir is:

$$Q_i = C_w(L + 1.8W)d^{1.5} \tag{19}$$

73

where: C_w = 2.3 (1.25 for SI)
        L = length of curb opening, ft (m)
        W = lateral width of depression, ft (m)
        d = depth at curb measured from the normal cross slope, ft (m), i.e., $d = TS_x$

The weir equation is applicable to depths at the curb approximately equal to the height of the opening plus the depth of the depression. Thus, the limitation on the use of equation (19) for a depressed curb-opening inlet is:

$$d \leq h + a/12 \quad (d \leq h + a \, , \, SI)$$

where: h = height of curb-opening inlet, ft (m)
        a = depth of depression, in (m)

Experiments have not been conducted for curb-opening inlets with a continuously depressed gutter, but it is reasonable to expect that the effective weir length would be as great as that for an inlet in a local depression. Use of equation (19) will yield conservative estimates of the interception capacity.

The weir equation for curb-opening inlets without depression (W = 0) becomes:

$$Q_i = C_w L d^{1.5} \tag{20}$$

The depth limitation for operation as a weir becomes:
$d \leq h$

Curb-opening inlets operate as orifices at depths greater than approximately 1.4h. The interception capacity can be computed by equation (21):

$$Q_i = C_o h L (2g d_o)^{0.5} = C_o A [2g(d_i - \frac{h}{2})]^{0.5} \tag{21}$$

where: C_o = orifice coefficient
            = 0.67
        h = height of curb-opening inlet, ft (m)
        d_o = effective head on the center of the orifice throat, ft (m)
        A = clear area of opening, ft^2 (m^2)
        d_i = depth at lip of curb opening, ft (m)
        h = height of curb-opening orifice, ft (m)
          = $TS_x + a/12$

Equation (21) is applicable to depressed and undepressed curb-opening inlets and the depth at the inlet includes any gutter depression.

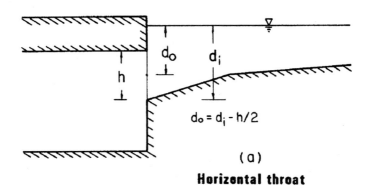

$do = d_i - h/2$

(a)

Horizontal throat

$$Q = 0.67 \, hL\sqrt{2\,g\,d_o}$$

L = LENGTH OF OPENING

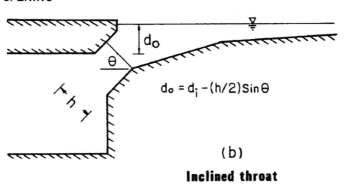

$d_o = d_i - (h/2)\sin\theta$

(b)

Inclined throat

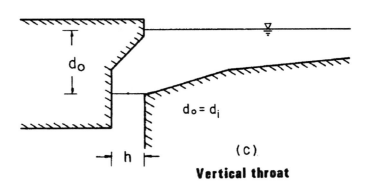

$d_o = d_i$

(c)

Vertical throat

Figure 21. Curb-opening inlets.

Height of the orifice in equation (21) assumes a vertical orifice opening. As illustrated in figure 21, other orifice throat locations can change the effective depth on the orifice and the dimension $(d_i - h/2)$. A limited throat width could reduce the capacity of the curb-opening inlet by causing the inlet to go into orifice flow at depths less than the height of the opening.

The orifice equation for curb-opening inlets with other than vertical faces (see figure 21) is:

$$Q = C_o hL(2gd_o)^{0.5} \tag{22}$$

where: $C_o = 0.67 =$ orifice coefficient
$h =$ orifice throat width, ft (m)
$d_o =$ effective head on the center of the orifice throat, ft (m)

Chart 12 provides solutions for equations (19) and (21) for depressed curb-opening inlets, and Chart 13 provides solutions for equations (20) and (21) for curb-opening inlets without depression. Chart 14 is provided for use for curb openings with other than vertical orifice throats.

Example 15 illustrates the use of Charts 12 and 13.

Example 15:

Given: Curb-opening inlet in a sump location
L = 5 ft
h = 5 in

(1) Undepressed curb opening
$S_x = 0.05$
T = 8 ft

(2) Depressed curb opening
$S_x = 0.05$
a = 2 in
W = 2 ft
T = 8 ft

Find: Q_i

Solution:
(1) $d = TS_x = 8 \times 0.05 = 0.4$ ft
d < h
$Q_i = 3.8$ ft^3/s   (Chart 13)

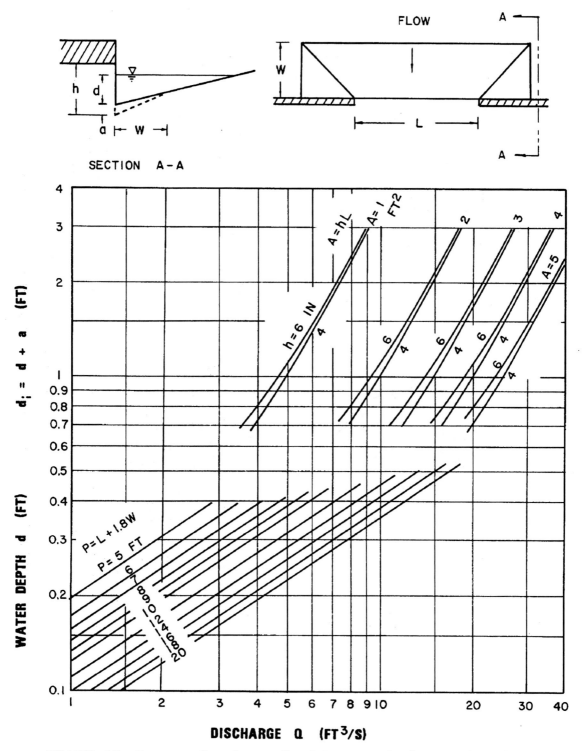

CHART 12. Depressed curb-opening inlet capacity in sump locations.

77

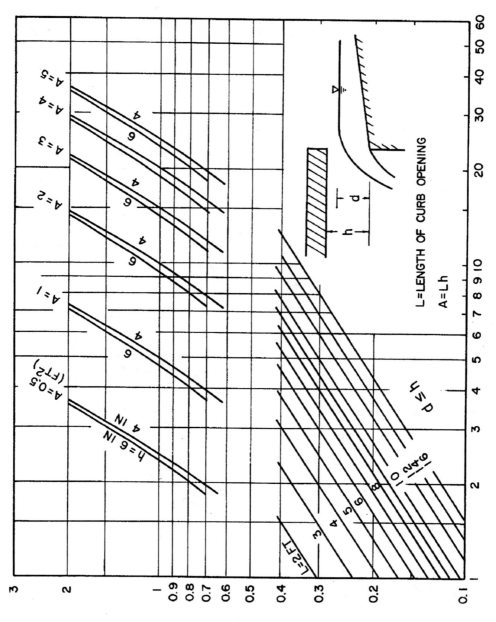

CHART 13. Curb-opening inlet capacity in sump locations.

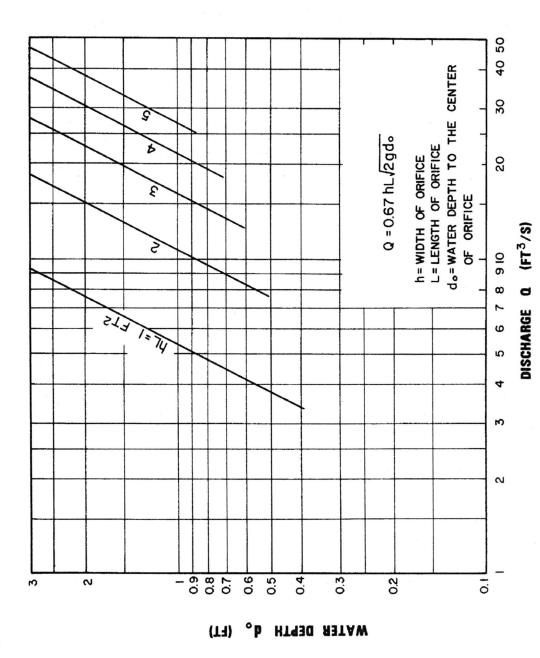

CHART 14. Curb-opening inlet orifice capacity for inclined and vertical orifice throats.

$$Q = 0.67\, hL\sqrt{2g d_0}$$

h = WIDTH OF ORIFICE
L = LENGTH OF ORIFICE
d_0 = WATER DEPTH TO THE CENTER
OF ORIFICE

DISCHARGE Q (FT³/S)

WATER DEPTH d_0 (FT)

79

        (2) d = 0.4 ft < (h + a/12)
            P = L + 1.8W = 5 + 3.6 = 8.6 ft

            Q_i = 5 ft^3/s (Chart 12)
    At a d = 0.4 ft, the depressed curb-opening inlet has about
30 percent more capacity than an inlet without depression. In
practice, the flow rate would be known and the depth at the curb
would be unknown.

8.3 Slotted Inlets

    Slotted inlets in sag locations perform as weirs to depths
of about 0.2 ft (0.06 m), dependent on slot width and length. At
depths greater than about 0.4 ft (0.12 m), they perform as
orifices. Between these depths, flow is in a transition stage.
The interception capacity of a slotted inlet operating as an
orifice can be computed by equation (23):

        Q_i = 0.8LW(2gd)$^{0.5}$ (23)

where: W = width of slot, ft (m)
        L = length of slot, ft (m)
        d = depth of water at slot, ft (m)
        d $\geq$ 0.4 ft (0.12 m)
        g = 32.16 ft/s/s (9.08 m/s/s)

    For a slot width of 1.75 in, equation (23) becomes:

        Q_i = 0.94Ld$^{0.5}$ (24)

    The interception capacity of slotted inlets at depths be-
tween 0.2 ft (0.06 m) and 0.4 ft (0.12 m) can be computed by use
of the orifice equation. The orifice coefficient varies with
depth, slot width, and the length of the slotted inlet.

    Chart 15 provides solutions for weir flow, equation (24),
and a plot representing data at depths between weir and orifice
flow.

Example 16:

Given: Q = 5 ft^3/s

Find: Length of slotted inlet required to limit maximum depth
        at curb to 0.3 ft, assuming no clogging

Solution:
        L = 15 ft (Chart 15)

80

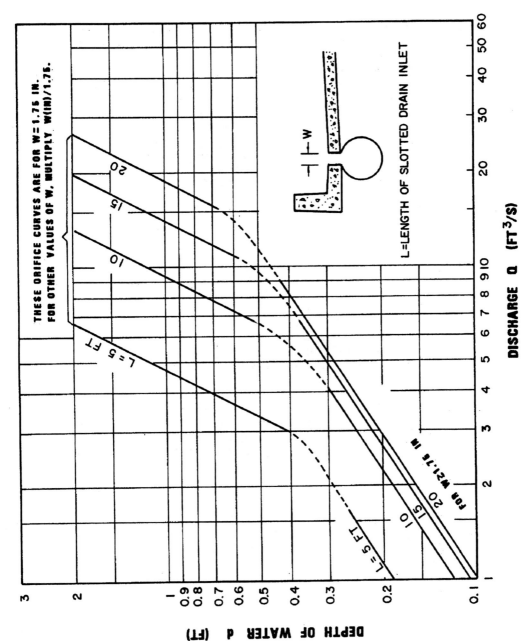

CHART 15. Slotted drain inlet capacity in sump locations.

THESE ORIFICE CURVES ARE FOR W=1.75 IN. FOR OTHER VALUES OF W, MULTIPLY W(IN)/1.75.

L=LENGTH OF SLOTTED DRAIN INLET

DISCHARGE Q (FT³/S)

DEPTH OF WATER d (FT)

8.4 Combination Inlets

Combination inlets consisting of a grate and a curb opening are considered advisable for use in sags where hazardous ponding can occur. The interception capacity of the combination inlet is essentially equal to that of a grate alone in weir flow unless the grate opening becomes clogged. In orifice flow, the capacity is equal to the capacity of the grate plus the capacity of the curb opening.

Equation (17) and Chart 11 can be used for weir flow in combination inlets in sag locations. Assuming complete clogging of the grate, equations (19), (20), and (21) and Charts 12, 13, and 14 for curb-opening inlets are applicable.

Where depth at the curb is such that orifice flow occurs, the interception capacity of the inlet is computed by adding equations (18) and (22):

$$Q_i = 0.67A_g(2gd)^{0.5} + 0.67hL(2gd_o)^{0.5} \tag{25}$$

where: A_g = clear area of the grate, ft^2 (m^2)
        g = 32.16 ft/s/s (9.08 m/s/s)
        d = depth at the curb, ft
        h = height of curb opening orifice, ft (m)
        L = length of curb opening, ft (m)
       d_o = effective depth at the center of the curb opening
            orifice, ft (m)

Trial and error solutions are necessary for depth at the curb for a given flow rate using Charts 11, 12 and 13 for orifice flow. Different assumptions for clogging of the grate can also be examined using these charts as illustrated by the following example.

Example 17:

Given: A combination inlet in a sag location.
         Grate: P - 1-7/8, 2 x 4 ft
         Curb opening: L = 4 ft, h = 4 in
         S_x = 0.03

         Q = 5 ft^3/s

Find: Depth at curb and spread for:
         (1) Grate clear of clogging
         (2) Grate 100 percent clogged

82

Solution:
```
        P = 2 + 2 + 4 = 8 ft
    (1) d = 0.36 ft  (Chart 11)
        T = d/S_x = 0.36/0.03 = 12 ft
```

$$P = 2 + 2 + 4 = 8 \text{ ft}$$
$$(1) \quad d = 0.36 \text{ ft} \quad (\text{Chart } 11)$$
$$T = d/S_x = 0.36/0.03 = 12 \text{ ft}$$

$$(2) \quad L = 4 \text{ ft}$$
$$A = 4 \times 0.33 = 1.33 \text{ ft}^2$$
$$d = 0.7 \text{ ft} \quad (\text{Chart } 13)$$
$$T = 0.7/0.03 = 23.3 \text{ ft}$$

Interception by the curb-opening only will be in a transition stage between weir and orifice flow with a depth at the curb of about 0.7 ft. Depth at the curb and spread on the pavement would be almost twice as great if the grate should become completely clogged.

9.0 INLET LOCATIONS

Pavement drainage inlet locations are often established by geometric features rather than by spread of water on the pavement and inlet interception capacity. In general, inlets should be placed at all low points in the gutter grade, at median breaks, intersections, and crosswalks, and on side streets at intersections where drainage would flow onto the highway pavement. Where pavement surfaces are warped, as at cross slope reversals and ramps, gutter flow should be intercepted in order keep the water from flowing across the pavement. Sheet flow across the pavement at these locations is particularly susceptible to icing. Inlets are also used upgrade of bridges to prevent pavement drainage from flowing onto bridge decks and downgrade of bridges to intercept drainage from the bridge.

Runoff from areas draining toward the highway pavement should be intercepted by roadside channels, where practicable, or inlets where open channels cannot be used. This applies to drainage from cut slopes, side streets, and other areas alongside the pavement. Curbed pavement sections and pavement drainage inlets are inefficient means for handling runoff and extraneous drainage should be intercepted before it reaches the highway pavement.

9.1 Inlet Spacing on Continuous Grades

The interception capacity of inlets on grade is discussed in sections 7.0 through 7.4. The location of inlets is determined by the criterion for spread on the pavement, geometric controls which require inlets at specific locations, and the use and location of flanking inlets in the sag. Thus, design spread on the pavement on grade becomes the criterion for locating inlets between inlets required by other considerations, and the flow which can be intercepted in the sag without hazardous ponding could become another consideration.

For a continuous slope, it is possible to establish the maximum design spacing between inlets of a given design if the drainage area consists of pavement only or has reasonably uniform runoff characteristics and is rectangular in shape. This assumes that the time of concentration is the same for all inlets. The following examples illustrate the effects of inlet efficiency on inlet spacing.

Example 18:

Given: 26 ft pavement width
         $n = 0.016$
         $S_x = 0.03$
         $S = 0.03$
         $T = 8$ ft
         $i = 10.7$ in/hr
         $C = 0.8$

Find: Maximum design inlet spacing for 2-ft by 2-ft curved vane
         grate

Solution:

$Q = CiA = 0.8 \times 10.7 \times 26 \times L/43,560 = 0.005L$

$\quad = 0.005$ ft^3/s/ft
$T = 8$ ft
$Q = 4.5$ ft^3/s   (Chart 3)

$L = \dfrac{Q}{0.005} = \dfrac{4.5}{0.005} = 900$ ft

The first inlet can be placed at 900 ft from the crest.

$W/T = 2/8 = 0.25;$
$S_w/S_x = 1$

$E_o = 0.54$ (Chart 4)
$V^o = 4.7$ ft/s (Chart 2)
$R_f = 1.0$ (Chart 7)
$R_s = 0.06$ (Chart 8)
$E = R_f E_o + R_s(1 - E_o) = 0.54 + 0.06(0.46) = 0.57$

$Q_i = EQ = 0.57(4.5) = 2.6$ ft^3/s

$Q_b = Q - Q_i = 4.5 - 2.6 = 1.9$ ft^3/s

The intervening drainage area between inlets should be
sufficient to generate runoff equal to the interception capacity
of the inlet, i.e., $Q_b + Q_i = Q$.

$Q = 0.005L$

$L = \dfrac{2.6}{0.005} = 520$ ft

Therefore, the initial inlet can be placed at 900 ft from
the crest and subsequent inlets at 520-ft intervals.

Example 19:

Given: Data from example 18.

Find: Maximum design inlet spacing for a 10-ft curb opening depressed 2-in from the normal cross slope in a 2-ft wide gutter.

Solution:

$Q = 4.5 \text{ ft}^3/\text{s}$ at initial inlet   (example 18)

$Q/S^{0.5} = 26.0$
$T = 6.6 \text{ ft}$ (figure 3)
$E_o = 0.76$ (Chart 4)
$S_e = S_w + S'_w E_o = 0.03 + (0.083)0.76 = 0.09$

$L_T = 20 \text{ ft}$ (Chart 9)

$L/L_T = 10/20 = 0.5$
$E = 0.7$ (Chart 10)
$Q_i = 4.5 \times 0.7 = 3.2 \text{ ft}^3/\text{s}$

$Q_b = 4.5 - 3.2 = 1.3 \text{ ft}^3/\text{s}$

The drainage area between inlets should contribute runoff equal to the interception capacity of the inlets.

$L = Q/0.005 = 3.2/0.005 = 640 \text{ ft}$

10-ft curb-opening inlets depressed 2-in can be spaced at 640 ft intervals.

Example 20:

Given: Data from example 18

Find: Maximum inlet spacing using a 15-ft slotted inlet

Solution:

$Q = 4.5 \text{ ft}^3/\text{s}$ (example 18)
$L_T = 38 \text{ ft}$ (Chart 9)

$L/L_T = 15/38 = 0.39$

$E = 0.59$ (Chart 10)
$Q_i = EQ = 0.59 \times 4.5 = 2.6 \text{ ft}^3/\text{s}$

$Q_b = 4.5 - 2.6 = 1.9 \text{ ft}^3/\text{s}$

L = 2.6/0.005 = 520 ft

15-ft slotted inlets can be spaced at 520-ft intervals.

In these examples, the first inlet could be placed at 900-ft downgrade from the crest. Curved vane grates could be spaced at 520-ft intervals, 10-ft depressed curb openings at 640-ft intervals, and 15-ft slotted inlets at 520-ft intervals. These results demonstrate the effects of the relative efficiencies of the selected inlet configurations for the chosen design conditions.

9.2 Inlets in Sag Locations

Sag vertical curves differ one from another in the potential for ponding, and criteria adopted for inlet spacing in sags should be applied only where traffic could be unduly disrupted if an inlet became clogged or runoff from the design storm were exceeded. Therefore, criteria adopted for inlet spacing in sag vertical curves are not applicable to the sag curve between two positive or two negative longitudinal slopes. Also, they should not be applied to locations where ponding depths could not exceed curb height and ponding widths would not be unduly disruptive, as in sag locations on embankment.

Where significant ponding can occur, in locations such as underpasses and in sag vertical curves in depressed sections, it is good engineering practice to place flanking inlets on each side of the inlet at the low point in the sag. The flanking inlets should be placed so that they will limit spread on low gradient approaches to the level point and act in relief of the inlet at the low point if it should become clogged or if the design spread is exceeded. Table 5 shows the spacing required for various depth at curb criteria and vertical curve lengths defined by K = L/A, where L is the length of the vertical curve and A is the algebraic difference in approach grades. The AASHTO policy on geometrics (2) specifies maximum K values for various design speeds.

Use of table 5 is illustrated in example 21.

Example 21:

Given: A sag vertical curve at an underpass on a 4-lane divided highway facility. Spread at design Q is not to exceed shoulder width of 10 ft.
S_x = 0.05
K = 130

Table 5. Distance to flanking inlets in sag vertical curve locations using depth at curb criteria.

| Speed | 20 | 25 | 30 | 35 | 40 | 45 | 50 | 55 | 60 | | 65 | 70 |
d \ K	20	30	40	50	70	90	110	130	160	167	180	220
0.1	20	24	28	32	37	42	47	51	57	58	60	66
0.2	28	35	40	45	53	60	66	72	80	82	85	94
0.3	35	42	49	55	65	73	81	88	98	100	104	115
0.4	40	49	57	63	75	85	94	102	113	116	120	133
0.5	45	55	63	71	84	95	105	114	126	129	134	148
0.6	49	60	69	77	92	104	115	125	139	142	147	162
0.7	53	65	75	84	99	112	124	135	150	153	159	176
0.8	57	69	80	89	106	120	133	144	160	163	170	188

Notes: $x = (200dK)^{0.5}$, where x = distance from the low point.
Drainage maximum $K = 167$

Find: Location of flanking inlets if located: (1) so that they will function in relief of the inlet at the low point when depth at the curb exceeds design depth, and (2) when depth at the curb is 0.2-ft less than depth at design spread.

Solution:
Depth at the curb at design spread,
$d = TS_x = 10 \times 0.05 = 0.5$ ft
(1) Spacing to flanking inlet = 114 ft (table 5)
(2) $d - 0.2$ ft = 0.5 - 0.2 = 0.3 ft
Spacing to flanking inlets = 88 ft (table 5)

Figure 22 illustrates the results of using the second criterion to locate the flanking inlets.

The purpose in providing table 5 is to facilitate the selection of criteria for the location of flanking inlets based on the ponding potential at the site, the potential for clogging of the inlet at the low point, design spread, design speeds, traffic volumes, and other considerations which may be peculiar to the site under consideration. A depth at curb criterion which does not vary with these considerations neglects consideration of cross slope and design spread and may be unduly conservative at some locations. Location of flanking inlets at a fixed slope rate on the vertical curve also neglects consideration of

speed facilities and not at all conservative for high speed
facilities.

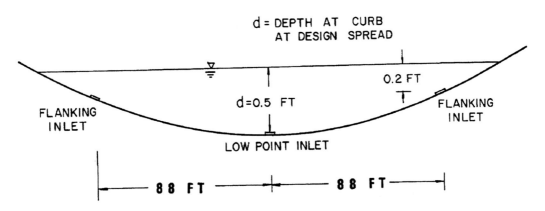

**Figure 22.   Example use of depth at curb criterion
to establish locations of flanking inlets.**

Example problem solutions in section 8 illustrate the total
interception capacity of inlets in sag locations. Except where
inlets become clogged, spread on low gradient approaches to the
low point is a more stringent criterion for design that the
interception capacity of the sag inlet. AASHTO ($\underline{2}$) recommends
that a gradient of 0.3 percent be maintained within 50 feet of
the level point in order to provide for adequate drainage. It is
considered advisable to use spread on the pavement at a gradient
comparable to that recommended by the AASHTO Committee on Design
to evaluate the location and design of inlets upgrade of sag
vertical curves. Standard inlet design and/or location may need
adjustment to avoid excessive spread in the sag curve.

Example 22:

Given: A 2-ft x 2-ft P - 1-7/8 grate is to be placed in a
         flanking inlet location in a sag vertical curve 250 ft
         downgrade from the inlet in example 18.

$$Q_b = 1.9 \ ft^3/s \ \text{(example 18)}$$
$$S_x = 0.03$$
$$T = 8 \ ft$$
$$n = 0.016$$

89

$$i = 10.7 \text{ in/hr}$$

Slope on the curve at the inlet, $S = 0.006$

Find: Spread at the flanking inlet and at $S = 0.003$

Solution:

$Q = 1.9 + 0.8(10.7)(26 \times 250)/43,560 = 3.2 \text{ ft}^3/\text{s}$

Spread at $S = 0.006$:

$T = 9.5 \text{ ft}$ (Chart 3)

$W/T = 2/9.5 = 0.21$

$E_o = 0.46$ (Chart 4)

$d = TS_x = 9.5 \times 0.03 = 0.28 \text{ ft}$

$A = 9.5 \times 0.28/2 = 1.33 \text{ ft}^2$

$V = Q/A = 3.2/1.33 = 0.24 \text{ ft/s}$

$R_f = 1.0$ (Chart 7)

$R_s = 0.5$ (Chart 8)

$E = R_f E_o + R_s(1 - E_o) = 1.0(0.46) + 0.5(0.54)$

$= 0.73$

$Q_i = EQ = 0.73 \times 3.2 = 2.3 \text{ ft}^3/\text{s}$

$Q_b = 3.2 - 2.3 = 0.9 \text{ ft}^3/\text{s}$

Spread at $S = 0.003$:

$T = 7 \text{ ft}$

Spread at the flanking inlet exceeds the design spread of 8 ft and spread from the bypass flow from the flanking inlet approaches design spread at the gradient of 0.3 percent. The design of the inlet upgrade could be modified to limit bypass flow to a lesser amount in order to reduce spread in the sag vertical curve, or the possibility of using a depressed gutter in the low gradient approaches to the low point could be investigated.

10.0 MEDIAN, EMBANKMENT, AND BRIDGE INLETS

Flow in median and roadside ditches is discussed in Hydraulic Engineering Circular No. 15 (15) and Hydraulic Design Series No. 4 (16). It is sometimes necessary to place inlets in medians at intervals to remove water that could cause erosion. Inlets are sometimes used in roadside ditches at the intersection of cut and fill slopes to prevent erosion downstream of cut sections.

Where adequate vegetative cover can be established on embankment slopes to prevent erosion, it is preferable to allow storm water to discharge down the slope with as little concentration of flow as practicable. Where storm water must be collected with curbs or swales, inlets are used to receive the water and discharge it through chutes, sod or riprap swales, or pipe downdrains.

Bridge deck drainage is similar to roadway drainage and deck drainage inlets are similar in purpose to roadway inlets. Bridge deck drainage is discussed in section 10.3.

10.1 Median and Roadside Inlets

The design of roadside and median channels involves the design of stable channels, safe roadsides, and the use of inlets to intercept flow that would erode the channels. Hydraulic Engineering Circular No. 15 (15) contains extensive discussion on the design of stable channels. The AASHTO Committee on Design Task Force on Hydrology and Hydraulics Highway Drainage Guidelines, Volume VI (17) also contains much useful information on the design of stable and safe roadside and median channels.

Safe roadsides have been the subject of much study and research. It is impractical to include a comprehensive discussion of roadside drainage design as related to roadside safety here, and it is improbable that this publication would become an authoritative source of information on the subject because of its principal focus on pavement drainage. The absence of discussion, however, should not be interpreted as a deemphasis on the importance of roadside safety. Authoritative information should be obtained by referring to current research reports and the latest publications on the subject by state highway agencies, the FHWA, AASHTO, and the Transportation Research Board (19, 20, 21). Roadside drainage designs can be made traffic safe where knowledge of the principals of safe roadsides is judiciously applied.

Medians may be drained by drop inlets similar to those used for pavement drainage, by pipe culverts under one roadway, or by cross drainage culverts which are not continuous across the median. Figure 23 illustrates a traffic-safe median inlet. Inlets, pipes, and discontinuous cross drainage culverts should be designed so as not to detract from a safe roadside. Drop inlets should be flush with the ditch bottom and traffic-safe grates should be placed on the ends of pipes used to drain medians that would be a hazard to errant vehicles. Cross drainage structures should be continuous across the median unless the median width makes this impractical. Ditches tend to erode at drop inlets; paving around the inlets helps to prevent erosion and may increase the interception capacity of the inlet marginally by acceleration of the flow.

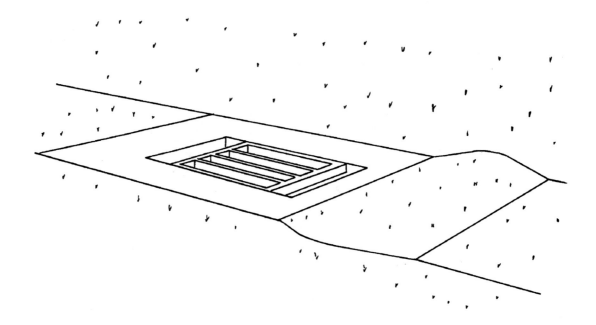

Figure 23. Median drop inlet.

Pipe drains for medians operate as culverts and generally require more water depth to intercept median flow than drop inlets. No test results are available on which to base design procedures for estimating the effects of placing grates on culvert inlets.

The interception capacity of drop inlets in median ditches on continuous grades can be estimated by use of Charts 16 and 17 to estimate flow depth and the ratio of frontal flow to total flow and Charts 7 and 8 to estimate the ratios of frontal and side flow intercepted to total flow.

Small dikes downstream of drop inlets (figure 23) insure complete interception of flow. The dikes usually need not be more than a few inches high and should have traffic safe slopes. The height of dike required for complete interception on .continuous grades or the depth of ponding in sag vertical curves can be computed by use of Chart 11. The effective perimeter of a grate in an open channel with a dike should be taken as 2(L + W) since one side of the grate is not adjacent to a curb. Use of Chart 11 is illus-trated in section 7.1.

The following examples illustrate the use of Charts 16, 17, 7, and 8 for drop inlets in ditches on continuous grade.

Example 23:

Given: A median ditch, B = 4 ft, n = 0.03, Z = 6, S = 0.02,

$Q = 10$ ft^3/s; flow in the median ditch is to be intercepted by a drop inlet with a 2-ft by 2-ft parallel bar grate; no dike will be used downstream of the grate.

Find: Q_i, Q_b

Solution:
$Qn = 10(0.03) = 0.3$ ft^3/s
$d/B = 0.11$ (Chart 16)
$d = 0.11 \times 4 = 0.44$ ft
$E_o = 0.30$ (Chart 17)
$A = 0.44[4 + (6 \times 0.44)] = 2.92$ ft^2
$V = Q/A = 10/2.92 = 3.4$ ft/s
$R_f = 1.0$ (Chart 7)
$R_s = 0.035$ (Chart 8)(since the ditch bottom is nearly flat, the least cross slope available on Chart 8 is used to estimate the ratio of side flow interception)
$E = R_f E_o + R_s(1 - E_o) = 1.0(0.30) + 0.035(0.70) = 0.32$

$Q_i = EQ = 0.32(10) = 3.2$ ft^3/s

$Q_b = 6.8$ ft^3/s

In the above example, a 2-ft drop inlet would intercept about 30 percent of the flow in a 4-ft bottom ditch on continuous

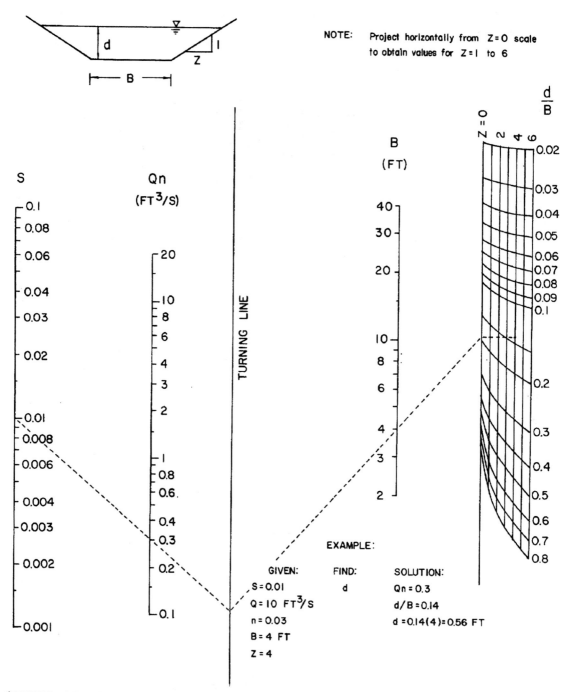

CHART 16. Solution of Manning's equation for channels of various side slopes.

94

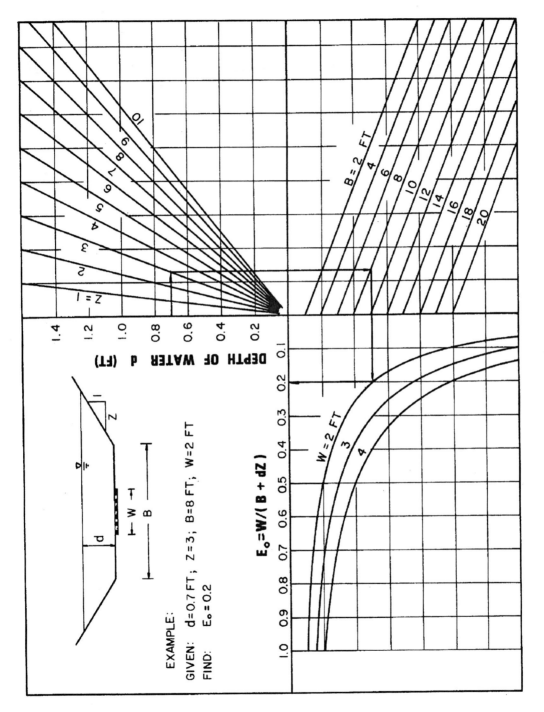

CHART 17. Ratio of frontal flow to total flow in a trapezoidal channel.

EXAMPLE:

GIVEN: d=0.7 FT ; Z=3 ; B=8 FT ; W=2 FT

FIND: E_o = 0.2

$E_o = W/(B + dZ)$

DEPTH OF WATER d (FT)

grade. Increased side interception would result from warping the bottom of the ditch to slope toward the drop inlet.

For grate widths equal to the bottom width of the ditch, use Chart 8 by substituting ditch side slopes for values of S_x, as illustrated in example 24.

Example 24:

Given: $Q = 10 \text{ ft}^3/s$
$B = 2 \text{ ft}$
$W = 2 \text{ ft}; L = 2 \text{ ft}$
$n = 0.03$
$Z = 6; S_x = 1/6 = 0.17$
$S = 0.03$
Use a P - 1-7/8 grate, 2 x 2 ft

Find: Q_i, Q_b

Solution:
$Qn = 0.3 \text{ ft}^3/s$
$d/B = 0.24$ (Chart 16)
$d = 0.24 \times 2 = 0.5 \text{ ft}$
$V = Q/A = 4 \text{ ft}/s$
$E_o = 0.4$ (Chart 17)
$R_f = 1.0$ (Chart 7)
$R_s = 0.3$ (Chart 8)
$E = 0.4 + 0.3(0.6) = 0.58$

$Q_i = 0.58 \times 10 = 5.8 \text{ ft}^3/s$

$Q_b = 4.2 \text{ ft}^3/s$

The height of dike downstream of a drop inlet required for total interception is illustrated by example 25.

Example 25:

Given: Data from example 24

Find: Required height of berm downstream of the grate inlet to cause total interception of flow in the ditch.

Solution:
$P = 2 + 2 + 2 + 2 = 8 \text{ ft}$ (flow can enter the grate from all sides)
$d = 0.5 \text{ ft}$ (Chart 11)

A dike will need to be 0.5 ft high for total interception.

If the grate should become partially clogged, transition or orifice flow could result and as much as 1.0 ft of head might be required.

10.2 Embankment Inlets

Drainage inlets are often needed to collect runoff from pavements in order to prevent erosion of fill slopes or to intercept water upgrade or downgrade of bridges. Inlets used at these locations differ from other pavement drainage inlets in three respects. First, the economies which can be achieved by system design are often not possible because a series of inlets is not used; secondly, total or near total interception is sometimes necessary in order to limit the bypass flow from running onto a bridge deck; and third, a closed storm drainage system is often not available to dispose of the intercepted flow, and the means for disposal must be provided at each inlet. Intercepted flow is usually discharged into open chutes or pipe downdrains which terminate at the toe of the fill slope.

Example problem solutions in other sections of this Circular illustrate by inference the difficulty in providing for near total interception on grade. Grate inlets intercept little more than the flow conveyed by the gutter width occupied by the grate and tandem installations of grates would possibly be the most practical way of achieving near total interception. Combination curb-opening and grate inlets can be designed to intercept total flow if the length of curb opening upstream of the grate is sufficient to reduce spread in the gutter to the width of the grate used. Depressing the curb opening would significantly reduce the length of inlet required. A combination inlet or tandem grate inlets would not usually be economical solutions to the need for near total interception, however. Perhaps the most practical inlets for use where near total interception is necessary are slotted inlets of sufficient length to intercept 85-100 percent of the gutter flow. Design charts and procedures in sections 7.1 to 7.4 are applicable to the design of inlets on embankments. Figure 24 illustrates a combination inlet and downdrain.

Downdrains or chutes used to convey intercepted flow from inlets to the toe of the fill slope may be open or closed chutes. Pipe downdrains are preferable because the flow is confined and cannot cause erosion along the sides, and because they can be covered to reduce or eliminate interference with maintenance operations on the fill slopes. Open chutes are often damaged by erosion from water splashing over the sides of the chute due to oscillation in the flow and from spill over the sides at bends in

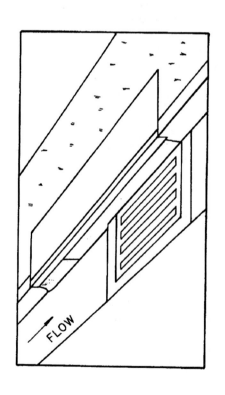

FLOW

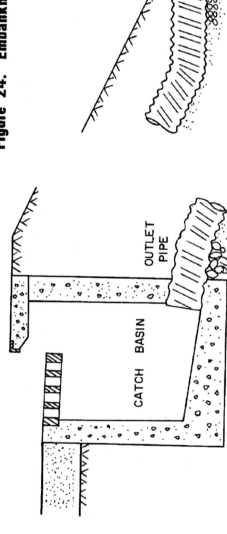

OUTLET PIPE

CATCH BASIN

Figure 24.   Embankment inlet and downdrain.

98

the chute. Erosion at the ends of downdrains or chutes is not usually a problem if the end of the device is placed low enough to prevent damage by undercutting. Small, localized scour holes are usually formed which serve as stilling basins. Well-graded gravel or rock can be used to control the size of the scour hole, if necessary.

10.3 Bridge Deck Inlets

Bridge deck drainage is regarded by many bridge engineers as a nuisance and a matter of continuing concern (21). Bridge deck drainage may be more than a nuisance, however, if the effects of icing on traffic safety and the corrosive effects of deicing agents on vehicles and structures are considered. Reference (21) is recommended for insight on the many problems associated with bridge deck drainage, and design measures that should be used to facilitate maintenance of bridge drainage systems. Bridge deck drainage could be improved immeasurably if cleaning of inlets and drainage systems were given a higher priority by maintenance personnel.

Bridge decks are possibly most effectively drained where the gradient is sufficient to convey water off the deck for interception. Dependent upon gradient, cross slope, and design spread, inlets can be omitted from many bridge decks if roadway drainage is intercepted upgrade of the bridge. The length of bridge deck that can be drained without inlets can be computed by runoff methods in section 4 and gutter flow methods in section 5. Example 18, section 9.1, illustrates the method that can be used to determine the length of bridge deck required for gutter flow to reach design spread.

The principles of inlet interception on bridge decks are the same as for roadway inlets. However, requirements in the design of deck drainage systems differ in the following respects from roadway drainage systems: (1) total or near total interception may be desirable upgrade of expansion joints; (2) deck drainage systems are highly susceptible to clogging; (3) inlet spacing is often predetermined by bent spacing, and (4) inlet sizes are often constrained by structural considerations. Figure 25 illustrates a grate inlet that represents about the maximum size inlet that can be used on many bridge decks.

It should be noted that small size inlets operate as orifices at lesser depths than inlets of larger dimensions. Experiments with 4-inch scuppers typically used on many bridges (22) show that scuppers of this size operate as orifices at depths of less than 0.1 ft on continuous grades. Interception

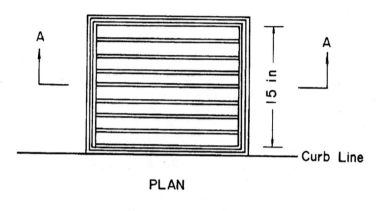

PLAN

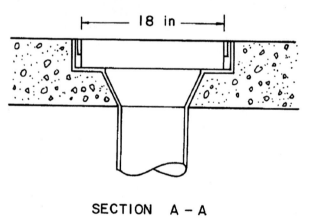

SECTION   A - A

Figure 25.   Bridge inlet.

capacities of small scuppers are extremely small, as illustrated by figure 26. Figure 27 is a plot of data for the same scupper drain in a sump condition.

Use of a safety factor should be considered in computing the interception capacity of bridge deck inlets because of their propensity to clog. It has been recommended that grate inlets should be twice the computed design size (21). This recommendation has application only at the low point in a sag vertical curve and structural constraints may not permit increasing the size of the inlet. A safety factor could be incorporated into designs, however, by considering clogging in computing inlet spacing.

Design charts included in sections 7.1 and 7.2 are applicable to inlets used on bridge decks. Short grate lengths have been included on Charts 7 and 8 to make the charts useful for the design of bridge deck inlets.

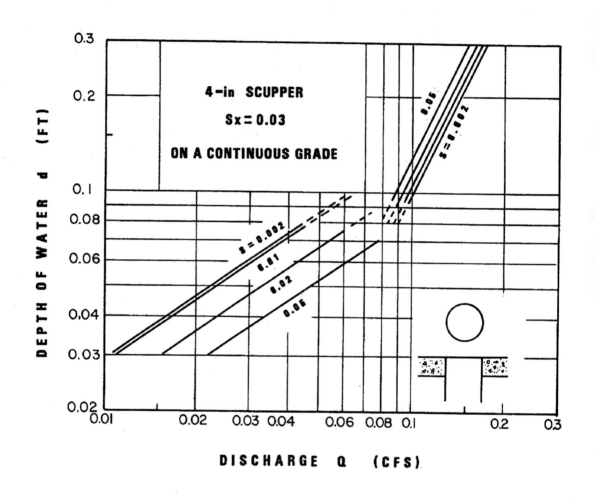

Figure 26. Interception capacity of 4–in scupper inlets on continuous grades.

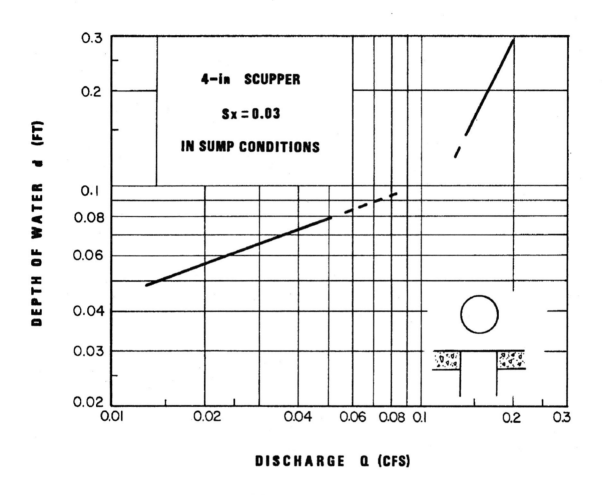

Figure 27. Capacity of 4-in scupper inlets in sump locations.

11.0 REFERENCES

(1)   Galloway, B.M., et al, "Pavement and Geometric Design
      Criteria for Minimizing Hydroplaning," Texas Transportation
      Institute, Texas A & M University, Federal Highway Adminis-
      tration, Report No. FHWA-RD-79-30, A Technical Summary,
      December 1979.

(2)   American Association of State Highway and Transportation
      Officials Subcommittee on Design, "A Policy on Geometric
      Design of Highways and Streets," Review Draft #4, American
      Association of State Highway and Transportation Officials,
      Washington, D.C., May 1983.

(3)   Burgi, P.H., D.E. Gober, "Bicycle-Safe Grate Inlets Study,
      Volume 1 - Hydraulic and Safety Characteristics of Selected
      Grate Inlets on Continuous Grades," Report No. FHWA-RD-77-
      24, Federal Highway Administration, June 1977.

(4)   Burgi, P.H., "Bicycle-Safe Grate Inlets Study, Volume 2 -
      Hydraulic Characteristics of Three Selected Grate Inlets on
      Continuous Grades," Report No. FHWA-RD-78-4, Federal High-
      way Administration, May 1978.

(5)   Burgi, P.H., "Bicycle-Safe Grate Inlets Study, Volume 3 -
      Hydraulic Characteristics of Three Selected Grate Inlets in
      a Sump Condition," Report No. FHWA-RD-78-70, Federal High-
      way Administration, September 1978.

(6)   Pugh, C.A., "Bicycle-Safe Grate Inlets Study, Volume 4 -
      Hydraulic Characteristics of Slotted Drain Inlets," Report
      No. FHWA-RD-79-106, Federal Highway Administration,
      February 1980.

(7)   Pugh, C.A., "Bicycle-Safe Grate Inlets Study, Volume 5 -
      Hydraulic Design of General Slotted Drain Inlets," Report
      No. FHWA-RD-80/081, Federal Highway Administration, October
      1980.

(8)   Chow, V.T., B.C. Yen, "Urban Stormwater Runoff: Deter-
      mination of Volume and Flowrates," EPA-600/2-76-116, Envi-
      ronmental Protection Agency, Cincinnati, Ohio, May 1976.

(9)   Chow, V.T., Editor-in-Chief, "Handbook of Applied Hydrol-
      ogy, A Compendium of Water Resources Technology," McGraw-
      Hill, New York, 1964.

(10) Jens, S.W., "Design of Urban Highway Drainage," FHWA-TS-79-225, Federal Highway Administration, August 1979.

(11) American Public Works Association Research Foundation and the Institute for Water Resources, "Urban Stormwater Management," Special Report No. 49, American Public Works Association, 1981.

(12) Joint Committee, American Society of Civil Engineers and the Water Pollution Control Federation, "Design and Construction of Sanitary and Storm Sewers," WPCF Manual of Practice No.9, ASCE Manuals and Reports on Engineering Practice, No. 37, American Society of Civil Engineers, Water Pollution Control Federation, 1970.

(13) Ragan, R.M., "A Nomograph Based on Kinematic Wave Theory for Determining Time of Concentration for Overland Flow," Report No. 44, prepared by Civil Engineering Department, University of Maryland at College Park, Maryland State Highway Administration and Federal Highway Administration, December 1971.

(14) Izzard, C.F., "Hydraulics of Runoff from Developed Surfaces," Proc. Highway Research Board, Volume 26, p. 129-150, Highway Research Board, Washington, D.C., 1946.

(15) Bauer, W.J. and Woo, D.C., "Hydraulic Design of Depressed Curb-Opening Inlets," Highway Research Record No. 58, Highway Research Board, Washington, D.C., 1964.

(16) Li, W.H., "The Design of Storm-Water Inlets," Johns Hopkins University, Baltimore, Maryland, June 1956.

(17) Normann, J.M., "Design of Stable Channels with Flexible Linings," Hydraulic Engineering Circular No. 15, Federal Highway Administration, October 1975.

(18) Searcy, J.K., "Design of Roadside Drainage Channels, Hydraulic Design Series No. 4," Federal Highway Administration, Washington, D.C., 1965.

(19) American Association of State Highway and Transportation Officials Select Committee on Highway Safety, "Highway Design and Operational Practices Related to Highway Safety," Second Edition, American Association of State Highway and Transportation Officials, Washington, D.C., 1974.

(20) Transportation Research Board, "Traffic-Safe and
      Hydraulically Efficient Drainage Practices," National
      Cooperative Highway Research Program Synthesis of Highway
      Practice 3, Transportation Research Board, Washington,
      D.C., 1969.

(21) American Association of State Highway and Transportation
      Officials Subcommittee on Design, Task Force on Hydrology
      and Hydraulics, "Guidelines for the Hydraulic Analysis and
      Design of Open Channels," Highway Drainage Guidelines -
      Volume VI, American Association of State Highway and Trans-
      portation Officials, Washington, D.C., 1979.

(22) Transportation Research Board, "Bridge Drainage Systems,"
      National Cooperative Highway Research Program Synthesis of
      Highway Practice 67, Transportation Research Board,
      Washington, D.C., 1979.

APPENDIX A. DEVELOPMENT OF RAINFALL INTENSITY CURVES
AND EQUATIONS

1. Precipitation Intensity-Duration-Frequency Curves

Precipitation intensity-duration-frequency (I-D-F) information is necessary for the specific locality in which the Rational Method for estimating runoff is to be used. The two examples which follow illustrate the development of I-D-F curves from HYDRO-35 and NOAA Atlas 2.

HYDRO-35

HYDRO-35 maps included in this Appendix as figures 28 through 33 are for 2-year and 100-year frequencies and durations of 5, 15 and 60 minutes. To estimate intensities for 10-minutes and 30-minutes, the following equations are provided:

$$10\text{-min value} = 0.59\ (15\text{-min value}) + 0.41\ (5\text{-min}) \qquad (26)$$

$$30\text{-min value} = 0.49\ (60\text{-min value}) + 0.51\ (15\text{-min}) \qquad (27)$$

Use equations (28) through (31) to compute values for return intervals intermediate to the 2-year and 100-year frequencies.

$$5\text{-yr} = 0.278\ (100\text{-yr}) + 0.674\ (2\text{-yr}) \qquad (28)$$

$$10\text{-yr} = 0.449\ (100\text{-yr}) + 0.496\ (2\text{-yr}) \qquad (29)$$

$$25\text{-yr} = 0.669\ (100\text{-yr}) + 0.293\ (2\text{-yr}) \qquad (30)$$

$$50\text{-yr} = 0.835\ (100\text{-yr}) + 0.146\ (2\text{-yr}) \qquad (31)$$

Example 26:

Given: Location - Charlotte, North Carolina

Develop: I-D-F Curve for 2- to 100-year frequencies

Step 1:   Read 5-min, 15-min and 60-min rainfall volume values for 2-yr and 100-yr frequencies from figures 28-33 (table 6):

Table 6. Rainfall volumes, 2- and 100-yr.

	5-min	15-min	60-min
2-yr	0.47	0.97	1.72
100-yr	0.81	1.75	3.60

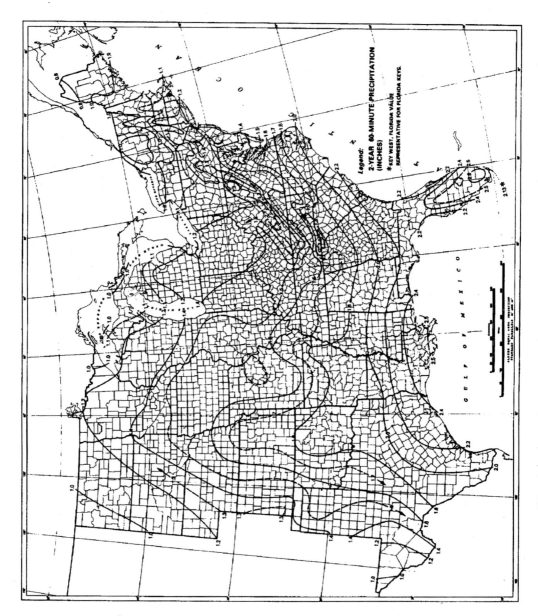

Figure 28. 2-year, 60-minute precipitation (HYDRO-35).

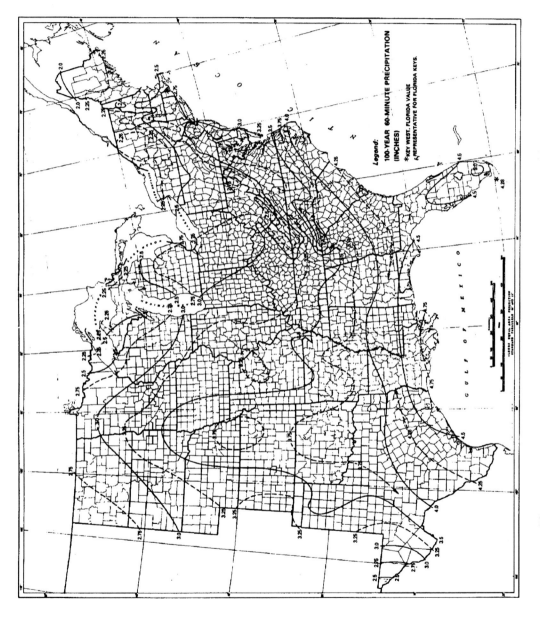

Figure 29. 100-year, 60-minute precipitation (HYDRO-35).

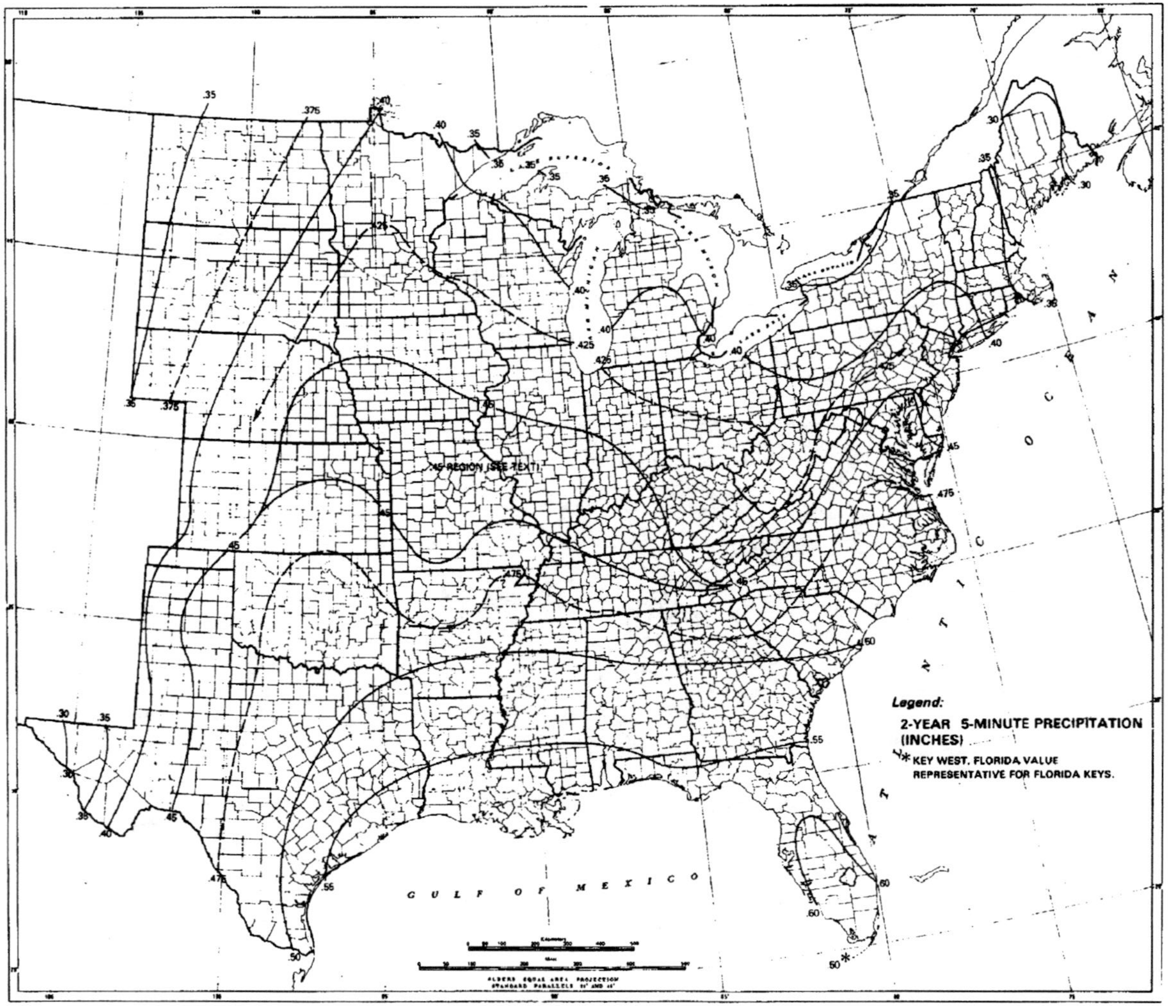

Figure 30. 2-year, 5-minute precipitation (HYDRO-35).

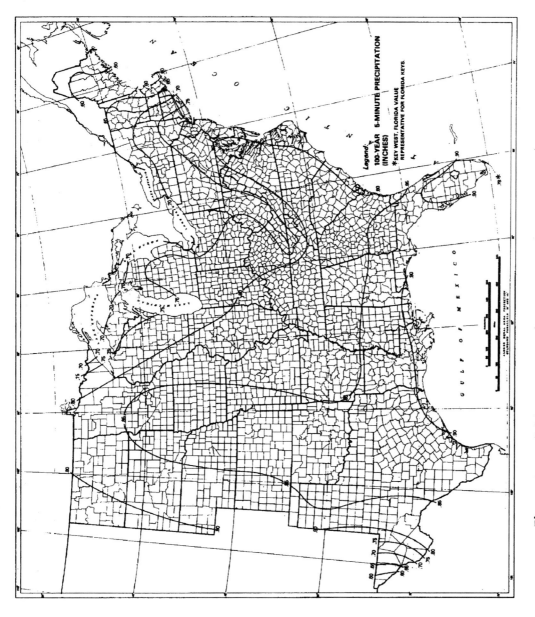

Figure 31. 100-year, 5-minute precipitation (HYDRO-35).

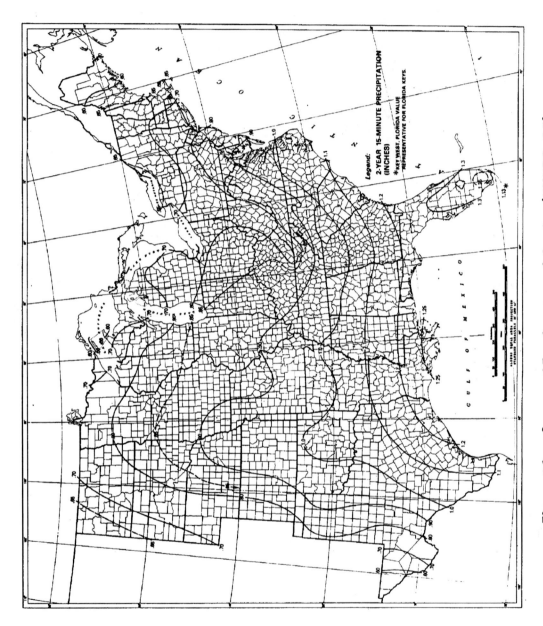

Figure 32.   2—year, 15—minute precipitation (HYDRO—35).

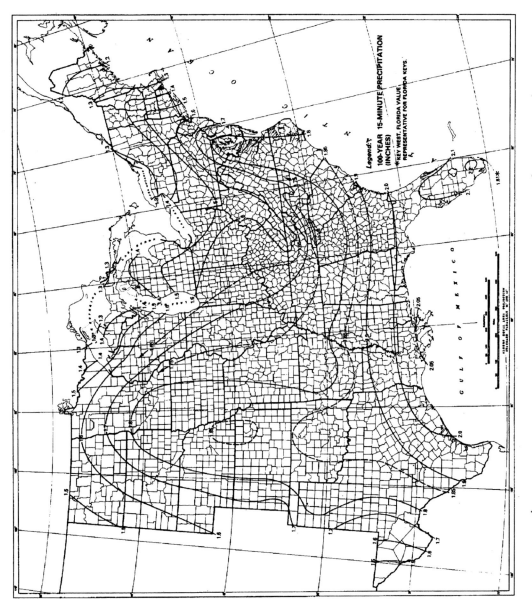

Figure 33. 100–year, 15–minute precipitation (HYDRO–35).

Step 2: Use equations (28) - (31) to compute 5-, 10-, 25-, and
         50-yr frequency values (table 7):

Table 7. Rainfall volumes, intermediate frequencies.

	5-min	15-min	60-min
5-yr	0.54	1.14	2.16
10-yr	0.60	1.27	2.47
25-yr	0.68	1.45	2.91
50-yr	0.74	1.60	3.26

Step 3: Use equations (26) and (27) to compute 10-min and 30-min
         values; complete table 8:

Table 8. Rainfall volumes.

	5-min	10-min	15-min	30-min	60-min
2-yr	0.47	0.76	0.97	1.34	1.72
5-yr	0.54	0.89	1.14	1.64	2.16
10-yr	0.60	1.00	1.27	1.86	2.47
25-yr	0.68	1.13	1.45	2.17	2.91
50-yr	0.74	1.25	1.60	2.41	3.26
100-yr	0.81	1.36	1.75	2.66	3.60

Step 4: Convert values in the table 8 to intensity in in/hr
         (table 9):

Table 9. I-D-F values, Charlotte, NC.

	5-min	10-min	15-min	30-mion	60-min
2-yr	5.64	4.56	3.88	2.68	1.72
5-yr	6.48	5.34	4.56	3.28	2.16
10-yr	7.2	6.00	5.08	3.72	2.47
25-yr	8.16	6.78	5.80	4.34	2.91
50-yr	8.88	7.50	6.40	4.82	3.26
100-yr	9.72	8.16	7.00	5.32	3.60

Step 5: Plot I-D-F Curve for Charlotte, North Carolina,
         figure 34.

114

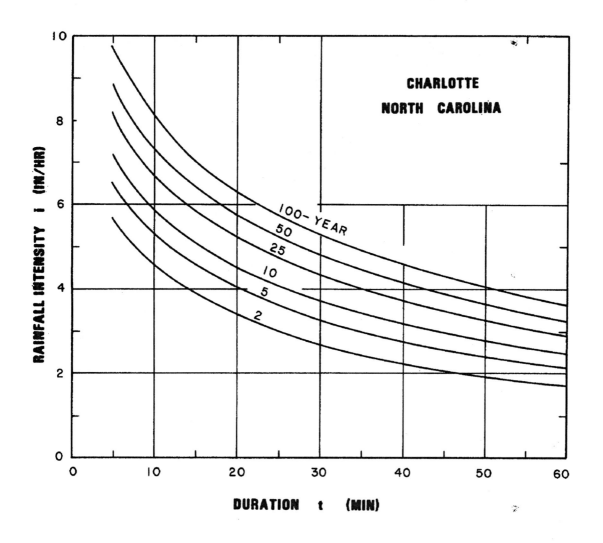

Figure 34. Intensity–duration–frequency curves for Charlotte, North Carolina.

Western Contiguous States

Isopluvials for 2-year and 100-year frequencies and 6-hour and 24-hour durations for the 11 western conterminous states are provided in the 11 volumes of NOAA Atlas 2. Volume III, Colorado, Geographic Region 1, is used here to illustrate the development of an I-D-F curve by the method in these publications.

Estimates for 1-hour duration precipitation are obtained by use of the following equations:

$$Y_2 = 0.218 + 0.709 \ [(X_1)(X_1/X_2)] \tag{32}$$

$$Y_{100} = 1.897 + 0.439 \ [(X_3)(X_3/X_4)] - 0.008z \tag{33}$$

where: Y_2 = 2-yr, 1-hr value
Y_{100} = 100-yr, 1-hr value
X_1 = 2-yr, 6-hr value from maps
X_2 = 2-yr, 24-hr value from maps
X_3 = 100-yr, 6-hr value from maps
X_4 = 100-yr, 24-hr value from maps
z = point elevation in hundreds of feet

A nomograph, figure 35, is provided for estimating precipitation amounts for return periods greater than 2 years and less than 100 years. To use the nomograph, draw a straight line between the 2-yr and 100-yr values and read the values for intermediate return periods. Use the ratios below to convert 1-hr rainfall volumes to volumes for lesser time periods:

Duration	5-min	10-min	15-min	30-min
Ratio to 1-hr	0.29	0.45	0.57	0.79

Example 27:

Given: Location – Colorado Springs, Colorado
Elevation – 6000 ft

Develop: I-D-F Curve

Step 1: Read 6-hour and 24-hour precipitation – frequency values from maps

	6-hr	24-hr
2-yr	1.75	2.1
100-yr	3.5	4.5

Step 2: Use Equations (32) and (33) to compute 1-hr rainfall for 2-yr and 100-yr frequency

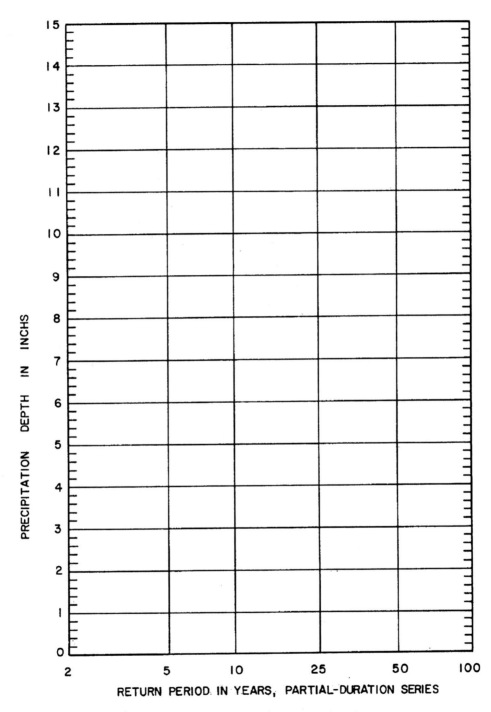

Figure 35. Nomograph for estimating precipitation amounts (Volume 3, NOAA Atlas 2).

$$Y_2 = 0.218 + 0.709[(1.75)(1.75/2.1)] = 1.25 \text{ inches}$$

$$Y_{100} = 1.897 + 0.439[(3.5)(3.5/4.5)] - 0.008 \ (60)$$
$$= 2.6 \text{ in}$$

Step 3: Estimate 1-hr precipitation amounts for 5, 10, 25 and 50-year return periods by use of figure 35. Draw a straight line between the 2-yr and 100-yr values to obtain values for intermediate return periods. (table 10):

Table 10. 1-hr rainfall volumes.

2-yr	5-yr	10-yr	25-yr	50-yr	100-yr
1.25	1.6	1.8	2.1	2.4	2.6

Step 4: Estimate precipitation amounts for durations of less than 1-hr using ratios provided above and convert to intensities (table 11):

Table 11. I-D-F values, Colorado Springs, Colorado.

	5	10	15	30	60
2-yr	4.4	3.4	2.8	2.0	1.25
5	5.6	4.3	3.6	2.5	1.6
10	6.3	4.9	4.1	2.8	1.8
25	7.3	5.7	4.8	3.3	2.1
50	8.4	6.5	5.5	3.8	2.4
100-yr	9.0	7.0	5.9	4.1	2.6

Step 5: Plot I-D-F Curves for Colorado Springs, Colorado, figure 36.

2. Development of Equations for Rainfall Intensity-Duration

It is sometimes necessary to develop equations for the rainfall intensity-duration curves for the various frequencies. This is especially useful for computer solutions of runoff rates. The equation for intensity curves is usually of the form:

$$i = \frac{a}{(t + b)^m} \tag{34}$$

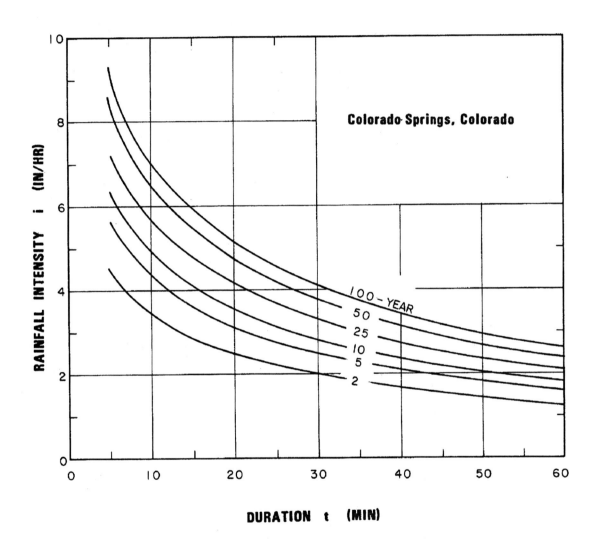

Figure 36. Intensity-duration-frequency curves for Colorado Springs, Colorado.

119

<u>Example 28</u>:

Given: Precipitation intensity vs duration data for 5-year recurrence interval for Charlotte, North Carolina

Duration (min)	5	10	15	30	60
Rainfall Intensity (in/hr)	6.48	5.34	4.56	3.28	2.16

Required: Develop an equation for rainfall intensity

Step 1: Make a table similar to table 12 with several columns
for trial and error solution and record the data in the
first 2 columns.

Table 12. I-D-F curve fitting table.

(1)	(2)	(3)	(4)	(5)	(6)	(7)
i	t	\multicolumn{3}{c}{Duration = t + b}		
in/hr	min	b = 5	b = 10	b = 12		
6.48	5	10	15	17		
5.34	10	15	20	22		
4.56	15	20	25	27		
3.28	30	35	40	42		
2.16	60	65	78	72		

Step 2: Plot the data (columns 1 and 2) on 2-cycle logarithmic
paper and draw a curve through the data points. Generally, the data points will not be on a straight line; if
the line is straight, go to Step 5. These data points
are plotted in figure 37.

Step 3: Add some constant value to column 2 and enter in column
3. For this example, b = 5 is used. Plot the values in
columns 1 and 3 in figure 37 and draw a curve through
the data points.

Step 4: If the data points are not on a straight line, change
the constant b and repeat step 3 until the data points
approximate a straight line.

Step 5: The value of a is then read as the ordinate at t = 1.
The value of m is the slope of the line. For this
example, b = 12, a = 57, and m = 0.77. Thus, the
equation for a 5-year recurrence interval is:

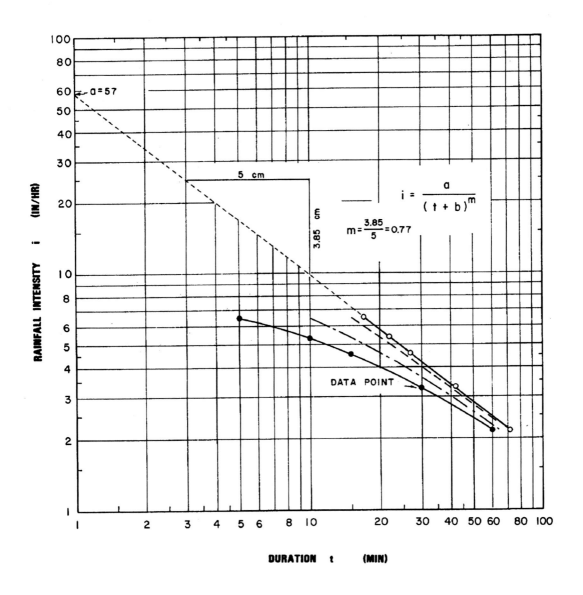

Figure 37. Development of precipitation intensity–duration equations.

121

$$i = \frac{57}{(t + 12)^{0.77}}$$

Step 6: Confirm the constants derived for the equation by checking against the original values of i. Adjust the constants as necessary.

Step 7: Repeat the procedure for other frequencies.

Flow time in curbed gutters is one component of the time of concentration for the contributing drainage area to the inlet. Velocity in a triangular gutter varies with the flow rate, and the flow rate varies with distance along the gutter, i.e., both the velocity and flow rate in the gutter are spatially varied. Figure 38 is a sketch of the concept used to develop average velocity in a reach of channel.

Time of flow can be estimated by use of an average velocity obtained by integration of the Manning equation for a triangular channel with respect to time. The assumption of this solution is that the flow rate in the gutter varies uniformly from Q_1 at the beginning of the section to Q_2 at the inlet.

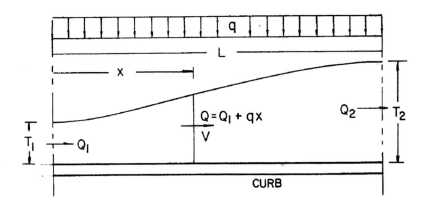

Figure 38. Conceptual sketch of spatially varied gutter flow.

$$Q = \frac{0.56}{n} S^{0.5} S_x^{1.67} T^{2.67} = K_1 T^{2.67} \tag{35}$$

$$K_1 = \frac{0.56}{n} S^{0.5} S_x^{1.67}$$

$$V = \frac{Q}{T^2 S_x/2} = \frac{1.12}{n} S^{0.5} S_x^{0.67} T^{0.67} = K_2 T^{0.67} \tag{36}$$

123

$$K_2 = \frac{1.12}{n} S^{0.5} S_x^{0.67}$$

From equation (35):

$$T^{0.67} = (Q/K_1)^{0.25} \tag{37}$$

Substituting equation (37) into equation (36) results in:

$$V = \frac{dx}{dt} = \frac{K_2}{K_1^{0.25}} Q^{0.25} \quad \text{or} \quad \frac{dx}{Q^{0.25}} = \frac{K_2}{K_1^{0.25}} dt \tag{38}$$

Here, $Q = Q_1 + qx$ and therefore $dQ = qdx$. Combining these with equation (38) and performing the integration, the following equation results:

$$t = 4/3 (Q_2^{0.75} - Q_1^{0.75}) \frac{K_1^{0.25}}{K_2 q} \tag{39}$$

Then, the average velocity, $\bar{V}$, can be computed by dividing the length, L, by time, t:

$$\bar{V} = L/t = \frac{3K_2 q}{4K_1^{0.25}} \left(\frac{L}{Q_2^{0.75} - Q_1^{0.75}} \right) \tag{40}$$

Upon substitution of $L = (Q_2 - Q_1)/q$ and $Q = K_1 T^{2.67}$, $\bar{V}$ becomes:

$$\bar{V} = (3/4) K_2 \frac{(T_2^{2.67} - T_1^{2.67})}{(T_2^2 - T_1^2)} \tag{41}$$

To determine spread, T_a, where velocity is equal to the average velocity, let $V = \bar{V}$:

$$K_2 T_a^{0.67} = 3/4 K_2 \frac{T_2^{2.67} - T_1^{2.67}}{T_2^2 - T_1^2} \tag{42}$$

which results in:

$$\frac{T_a}{T_2} = 0.65 \left[\frac{1 - (T_1/T_2)^{2.67}}{1 - (T_1/T_2)^2} \right]^{1.5} \tag{43}$$

124

Solving equation (43) for values of T_1/T_2 gives results shown in the table below.

Spread at average velocity in a reach of triangular gutter.

T_1/T_2	Ø	0.1	0.2	0.3	0.4	0.5	0.6	0.7	0.8	0.9	1.0
T_a/T_2	0.65	0.66	0.68	0.70	0.74	0.77	0.82	0.86	0.91	0.95	1.0

The average velocity in a triangular channel can be computed by using the above table to solve for the spread, T_a, where the average velocity occurs. Where the initial spread is zero, average velocity occurs where the spread is 65 percent of the spread at the downstream end of the reach.

APPENDIX C. DEVELOPMENT OF SPREAD-DISCHARGE RELATIONSHIP FOR COMPOUND CROSS SLOPES.

The computations needed to develop charts relating spread to conveyance for a gutter section are not original with this Circular. The purpose for including the procedure, as well as the procedure for developing charts for parabolic sections, is to encourage agencies to develop charts for sections which they use as standards.

Computations for the development of charts involves dividing the channel into two sections at the break in cross slope and use of the integrated form of the Manning equation to compute the conveyance in each section. Total conveyance in the channel is equal to the sum of the parts. Following is a step by step procedure for the computations.

$$Q = \frac{0.56}{n}S_x^{1.67}S^{0.5}T^{2.67} \tag{4}$$

$$= \frac{0.56S^{0.5}d^{2.67}}{nS_x}$$

Example 29:

Given: W = 2 ft
           a = 2 in
           T = 6 ft
           S_x = 0.04

           $K = Q/S^{0.5}$

Required: Develop K - T relationship

Procedure:

Step 1:   Compute d_1 and d_2 where d_1 is the depth of flow at the break in the cross slope and d_2 is the depth at the curb (See sketch, Chart 4)

           $d_2 = (T - W)S_x = (6 - 2)0.04 = 0.16$

           $d_1 = TS_x + a = 6(0.04) + 0.167 = 0.407$

126

Step 2:   Compute conveyance in section outside of gutter

$$\frac{Q_s}{S^{0.5}} = \frac{0.56 d_2^{2.67}}{n S_x}$$

$$= \frac{0.56 \times 0.16^{2.67}}{0.016 \times 0.04} = 6.56 \text{ ft}^3/s$$

Step 3:   Compute conveyance in the gutter

$$\frac{Q_w}{S^{0.5}} = \frac{0.56 (d_1^{2.67} - d_2^{2.67})}{n S_w}$$

$$= \frac{0.56 (0.407^{2.67} - 0.16^{2.67})}{0.016 (0.0833 + 0.04)}$$

$$= 23.61 \text{ ft}^3/s$$

Step 4:   Compute total conveyance by adding results from Steps 2 and 3.

6.56 + 23.61 = 30.18 ft^3/s

Step 5:   Repeat Steps 1 through 4 for other widths of spread, T.

Step 6:   Repeat Steps 1 through 5 for other cross slopes, S_x.

Step 7:   Plot curves of K - T relationship as shown in figure 3, section 5.2.

APPENDIX D. DEVELOPMENT OF SPREAD-DISCHARGE RELATIONSHIP FOR
PARABOLIC CROSS SECTIONS

A parabolic cross section can be described by the equation:

$$y = ax - bx^2 \tag{44}$$

where: $a = 2H/B$

$b = H/B^2$
H = crown height, ft (m)
B = half width, ft (m)

The relationships between a, b, crown height, H, and half
width, B, are shown in figure 39.

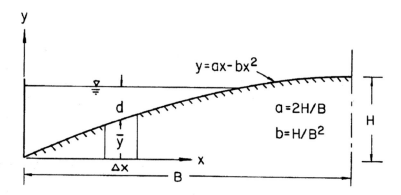

Figure 39. Properties of a parabolic curve

To determine total gutter flow, divide the cross section
into segments of equal width and compute the discharge for each
segment by Manning's equation. The parabola can be approximated
very closely by 2 ft (0.61 m) chords. The total discharge will
be the sum of the discharges in all segments.

The crown height, H, and half width, B, vary from one design
to another. Since discharge is directly related to the configuration of the cross section, discharge-depth (or spread) relationships developed for one configuration are not applicable for
roadways of other configurations. For this reason, the relationships must be developed for each roadway configuration.

The following procedure illustrates the development of a
conveyance curve for a parabolic pavement section with a half
width, B = 24 ft (7.32 m) and a crown height, H = 0.48 ft (0.15
m). The procedure is presented with reference to table 13.
Conveyance computations for spreads of 2 ft, 4 ft and 6 ft are
shown for illustration purposes.

Procedure:

Column 1: Choose the width of segment, Δx, for which the vertical
rise will be computed and record in column 1.

Column 2: Compute the vertical rise using equations (44) - (46).
For H = 0.48 ft and B = 24 ft, equation (44) becomes:

$$y = 0.04x - 0.0083x^2$$

Column 3: Compute the mean rise, $\bar{y}$, of each segment and record
in column 3.

Column 4: Depth of flow at the curb, d, for a given spread, T, is
equal to the vertical rise, y, shown in column 2. The
average flow depth for any segment is equal to depth at
the curb for the spread minus the mean rise in that
segment. For example, depth at curb for a 2 ft spread
is equal to 0.0767 ft. The mean rise in the segment is
equal to 0.0384 ft. Therefore, average flow depth in
the segment, d = 0.767 - 0.0384 = 0.0383. This will be
further illustrated for column 6.

Column 5: Conveyance for a segment can be determined from the
equation:

$$K = \frac{1.49}{n}Ad^{2/3} = \frac{1.49}{n}(\Delta x)(d)^{5/3} = \frac{1.49}{n}(2)d^{5/3}$$

Only "d" in the above equation varies from one segment
to another. Therefore, the equation can be operated on

with a summation of $d^{5/3}$.

Column 6: Average flow depth in the first 2 ft segment nearest
the curb is equal to the depth at the curb minus the
average rise in the segment,
$d = y - \bar{y} = 0.1467 - 0.0384 = 0.1083$ ft.
Similarly, the average flow depth in the second 2 ft
segment away from the curb is:
$d = 0.1467 - 0.1117 = 0.0350$ ft

Table 13. Conveyance computations, parabolic street section.

Dist. from Curb	Vert Rise y, ft	Ave. Rise $\bar{y}$	T = 2 ft* Ave.Flow Depth, d	$d^{5/3}$	T = 4 ft** Ave.Flow Depth, d	$d^{5/3}$	T = 6 ft*** Ave.Flow Depth, d	$d^{5/3}$
(1)	(2)	(3)	(4)	(5)	(6)	(7)	(8)	(9)
0	0							
		.0384	.0383	.0043	.1083	.0244	.1716	.0527
2*	0.0767							
		.1117			.0350	.0037	.0983	.0208
4**	.1467							
		.1784					.0316	.0031
6***	.2100							
		.2384						
8	.2667							
		.2917						
10	.3167							
		.3384						
12	.3600							
		.3784						
14	.3967							
		.4118						
16	.4268							
		.4385						
18	.4501							
		.4585						
20	.4668							
		.4718						
22	.4768							
		.4784						
24	.48							
Σ				.0043		.0281		.0766
$Q/S^{0.5}$ =			0.8		5.23		14.27	

$$Q = KS^{0.5} = \frac{1.49}{n}AR^{0.67}S^{0.5}$$

$$K = \frac{1.49}{n}(\Delta x)\,d^{1.67}$$

For n = 0.016 and Δx = 2 ft:

$$K = \frac{Q}{S^{0.5}} = (186.25)\,d^{1.67}$$

130

Columns 7, 8 and 9 are computed in the same manner as columns 4, 5 and 6.

The same analysis is repeated for other spreads equal to the half section width or for depths equal to the curb height, for curb heights <H.

Results of the analyses for spreads of 8 to 24 ft are shown in table 14:

Table 14.   Conveyance vs spread, parabolic street section.

T	8	10	12	14	16	18	20	22	24
d	.267	.317	.360	.397	.427	.450	.467	.477	.480
K	27.53	44.71	64.45	85.26	105.54	123.63	137.98	147.26	150.49

The results of the computations are plotted in figure 40. For a given spread or flow depth at the curb, the conveyance can be read from the figure and the discharge computed from the

equation, $Q = KS^{0.5}$. For a given discharge and longitudinal slope, the flow depth or spread can be read directly from the

figure by first computing the conveyance, $K = Q/S^{0.5}$, and using this value to enter the figure. An example is given on figure 40.

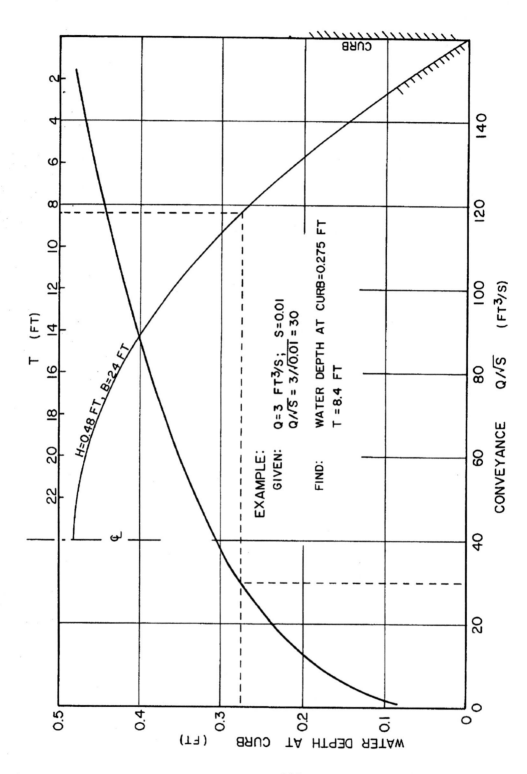

Figure 40. Conveyance curve for a parabolic cross section.

132

APPENDIX E. DEVELOPMENT OF DESIGN CHARTS FOR GRATE INLETS

The following step-by-step procedure may be used to develop design curves relating intercepted flow and total gutter flow, with spread as the third variable, for a given roadway geometry, grate type and size.

Example 30:

Given: $S_x = 0.04$

Grate - Type: P - 1-1/8
Size: 2 x 2 ft (W x L)
n = 0.016

Required: Develop design curves relating intercepted flow, Q_i, to total gutter flow, Q, for various spread widths, T. Intercepted flow is a function of total gutter flow, cross slope, and longitudinal slope, S. A discharge of

3 ft^3/s and longitudinal slope of 0.01 are used here to illustrate the development of curves.

Procedure:

Step 1: Determine spread, T, by use of Chart 3 or the following form of equation 4:

$$T = [\frac{nQ}{0.56S^{0.5}}]^{0.375}/S_x^{0.625}$$

For this example, with S = 0.01,

$$T = [\frac{3}{35(0.01)^{0.5}}]^{0.375}/(0.04)^{0.625} = 7.08 \text{ ft}$$

Step 2: Determine the ratio, E_o, of the frontal flow to total flow from Chart 4.

W/T = 2/7.08 = 0.28

$E_o = 0.59$

Step 3: Determine the mean velocity from Chart 2.

V = 3 ft/s

Step 4:   Determine the frontal flow interception efficiency, R_f, using Chart 7.

          $R_f = 1.0$

Step 5:   Determine the side flow interception efficiency, R_s, using Chart 8.

          $R_s = 0.15$

Step 6:   Compute the inlet interception efficiency by using equation (11).

          $E = R_f E_o + R_s(1 - E_o) = 1 \times 0.59 + 0.15(1 - 0.59)$

             $= 0.65$

Step 7:   Compute the intercepted flow.

          $Q_i = EQ = 0.65(3) = 1.95$ cfs

Step 8:   Repeat steps 1 through 7 for other longitudinal slopes

          to complete the design curve for $Q = 3$ ft^3/s.

Step 9:   Repeat steps 1 through 8 for other flow rates. Curves for the grate and cross slope selected for this illustration are shown in figures 41 and 42.

     Design curves for other grate configurations, roadway cross slopes, and gutter configurations can be developed similarly.

134

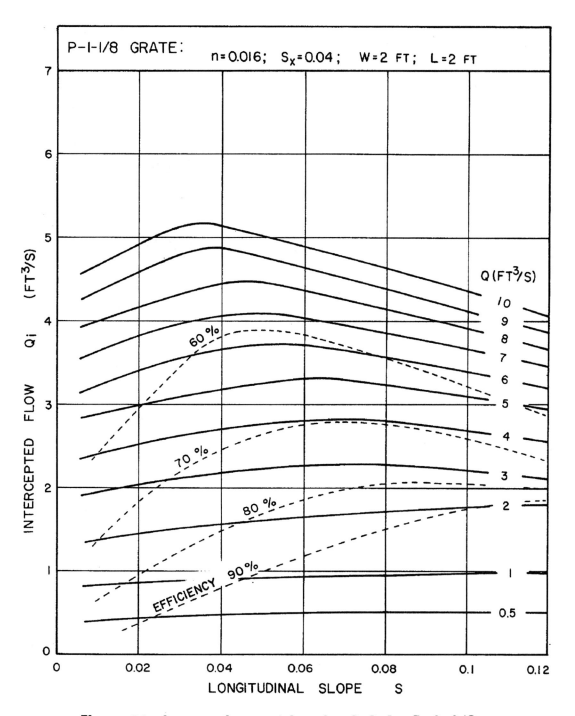

Figure 41. Interception capacity of a 2x2-ft, P–1–1/8 grate.

135

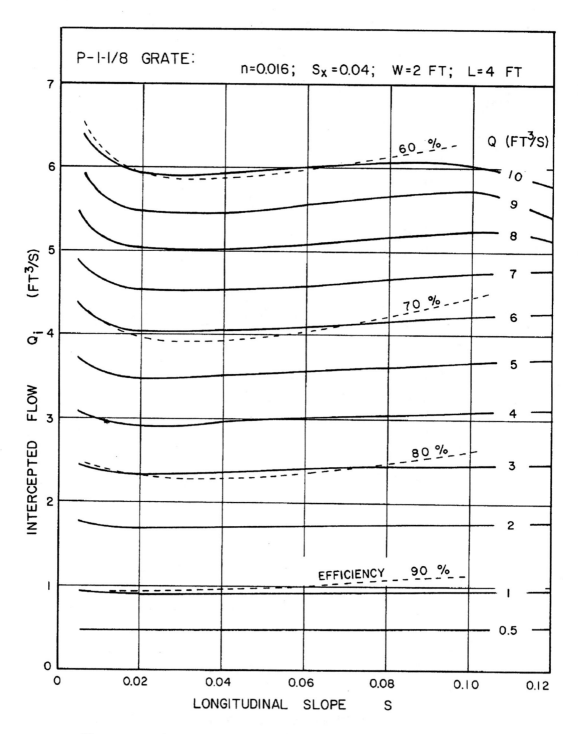

Figure 42. Interception capacity of a 2x4-ft, P-1-1/8 grate.

136

FEDERAL HIGHWAY ADMINISTRATION

Publications listed below are not available from the Government Printing
Office. These publications are available in limited numbers to State
highway agencies and other public agencies from the Federal Highway
Administration. Requests for these documents and suggestions on the
contents of any publications should be addressed to the Federal Highway
Administration, Office of Engineering, Bridge Division, HNG-31,
Washington, D.C. 20590

Hydraulic Design Series
HDS No. 1   HYDRAULICS OF BRIDGE WATERWAYS - Second Edition - Revised 1978
HDS No. 3   DESIGN CHARTS FOR OPEN-CHANNEL FLOW - 1961, Reprinted 1973
HDS No. 4   DESIGN OF ROADSIDE DRAINAGE CHANNELS - 1965

Hydraulic Engineering Circulars
HEC No. 1   SELECTED BIBLIOGRAPHY OF HYDRAULIC AND HYDROLOGIC SUBJECTS -
            July 1983
HEC No. 3   HYDROLOGY OF A HIGHWAY STREAM CROSSING - January 1961
HEC No. 5   HYDRAULIC CHARTS FOR THE SELECTION OF HIGHWAY CULVERTS -
            December 1965
HEC No. 9   DEBRIS-CONTROL STRUCTURES - March 1971
HEC No. 10 CAPACITY CHARTS FOR THE HYDRAULIC DESIGN OF HIGHWAY CULVERTS -
            November 1972
HEC No. 11 USE OF RIPRAP FOR BANK PROTECTION - June 1967
HEC No. 12 DRAINAGE OF HIGHWAYS PAVEMENTS - March 1969
HEC No. 13 HYDRAULIC DESIGN OF IMPROVED INLETS FOR CULVERTS - August 1972
HEC No. 14 HYDRAULIC DESIGN OF ENERGY DISSIPATORS FOR CULVERTS AND
            CHANNELS - December 1975
HEC No. 15 DESIGN OF STABLE CHANNELS WITH FLEXIBLE LININGS - October 1975
HEC No. 16 ADDENDUM TO HIGHWAYS IN THE RIVER ENVIRONMENT - HYDRAULIC AND
            ENVIRONMENTAL DESIGN CONSIDERATIONS - JULY 1980
HEC No. 17 THE DESIGN OF ENCROACHMENTS ON FLOOD PLAINS USING RISK ANALYSIS -
            October 1980

Electronic Computer Programs
HY-2   HYDRAULIC ANALYSIS OF PIPE-ARCH CULVERTS - May 1969
HY-4   HYDRAULICS OF BRIDGE WATERWAYS - 1969
HY-6   HYDRAULIC ANALYSIS OF CULVERTS (Box and Circular) - 1979

Calculator Design Series
CDS No. 1   HYDRAULIC DESIGN OF IMPROVED INLETS FOR CULVERTS USING
            PROGRAMABLE CALCULATORS, (COMPUCORP 325) - October 1980
CDS No. 2   HYDRAULIC DESIGN OF IMPROVED INLETS FOR CULVERTS USING
            PROGRAMABLE CALCULATORS, (HP-65) - October 1980
CDS No. 3   HYDRAULIC DESIGN OF IMPROVED INLETS FOR CULVERTS USING
            PROGRAMABLE CALCULATORS, (TI-59) - January 1981
CDS No. 4   HYDRAULIC ANALYSIS OF PIPE-ARCH AND ELLIPTICAL SHAPE
            CULVERTS USING PROGRAMABLE CALCULATORS, (TI-59) - March 1982
CDS No. 5   HYDRAULIC DESIGN OF STORMWATER PUMPING STATIONS USING
            PROGRAMABLE CALCULATORS, (TI-59), May 1982

CPSIA information can be obtained at www.ICGtesting.com
Printed in the USA
BVOW01s1516070214

344280BV00007B/284/P